NATIONAL AUDUBON SOCIETY®

FIRST
FIELD
GUIDE

REPTILES

NATIONAL AUDUBON SOCIETY®

FIRST FIELD GUIDE

REPTILES

Written by
John L. Behler

Scholastic Inc.

New York Toronto London Auckland Sydney
Mexico City New Delhi Hong Kong

The National Audubon Society, established in 1905, has 550,000 members and more than 500 chapters nationwide. Its mission is to conserve and restore natural ecosystems, focusing on birds and other wildlife, and these guides are part of that mission. Celebrating the beauty and wonders of nature, Audubon looks toward its second century of educating people of all ages.

For information about Audubon membership, contact:

National Audubon Society

700 Broadway

New York, NY 10003-9562

212-979-3000   800-274-4201

http://www.audubon.org

Copyright © 1999 by Chanticleer Press, Inc.
All rights reserved. Published by Scholastic Inc.
SCHOLASTIC and associated logos are trademarks and/or registered trademarks of Scholastic Inc.

LIBRARY OF CONGRESS CATALOGING-IN-PUBLICATION DATA
Behler, John L.
    National Audubon Society first field guide. Reptiles / by John
    Behler.
        p.   cm.
    Includes bibliographical references (p.   ) and index.
    Summary: Explores the world of reptiles, discussing their
subspecies and races, anatomy, behavior, and habitat and providing
photographs and detailed descriptions of individual species.
    ISBN 0-590-05467-8. (hc) — ISBN 0-590-05487-2 (pbk.)
    1. Reptiles—Juvenile literature. [1. Reptiles.] I. Title
II. Title: Reptiles.
QL644.2.B44   1999
597.9—DC21   98-8332

10 9 8 7 6 5 4 3 2 1   9/9   0/0   01   02   03

Printed in Hong Kong
First printing, April 1999

Contents

About this book

Blue Spiny Lizard

Whether you are watching reptiles in your own backyard, while picnicking near a pond, or during a trip to the desert, this book will help you learn to look at reptiles the way a naturalist does. The book is divided into four parts:

PART 1: The world of reptiles gives you lots of interesting information about reptiles, such as how they are named, what makes them perfectly suited to a variety of water and land habitats, and what these incredibly diverse creatures have in common.

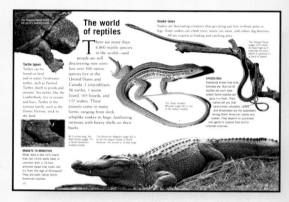

PART 2: How to look at reptiles tells you what you need to know to begin identifying reptiles—including what they look like, how they eat, move, and produce young, and where they live—as well as how to avoid dangerous reptiles.

PART 3: The field guide includes detailed descriptions, range maps, and dramatic photographs of 50 common North American reptiles. In addition, this section provides helpful shorter descriptions accompanied by photographs of more than 120 other important species and subspecies.

PART 4: The reference section at the back of the book includes a helpful glossary of terms used by naturalists when they talk about reptiles; lists of useful books, Web sites, and organizations; and an index of species covered in the field guide.

What is a naturalist?

A naturalist is a person who explores the world of nature. Some naturalists devote themselves to a particular part of nature, such as birds, snakes, or trees. A person who studies reptiles and amphibians is called a herpetologist. This unusual word comes from the Greek language and means a person who studies things that crawl.

Edward Drinker Cope (1840–1897), of Philadelphia's Academy of Natural Sciences, was one of North America's first herpetologists. He wrote hundreds of papers about reptiles and amphibians.

Explorer naturalists

In North America, the study of reptiles and amphibians grew from expeditions in the 1800s that crisscrossed the continent. Naturalists, doctors, and geologists who went on these explorations returned with collections of animals they had found. Many reptiles were described and named by these collectors and their colleagues at museums.

YOU CAN BE A NATURALIST, TOO!

Most herpetologists begin their careers as young naturalists who explore the ponds, fields, and woods around them and become fascinated with the lives of reptiles and amphibians. Next time you see a turtle, take a good look at it, then close your eyes and see if you can answer the following questions: What color was it? What shape was its shell? What was it doing? These are the kinds of questions that naturalists ask. They use their senses and their curiosity to learn about nature.

A herpetologist's tools

Very little equipment is needed to observe and enjoy reptiles and amphibians. A compact pair of binoculars is helpful for looking at basking lizards, snakes, and turtles. Take a small notebook and a pen or pencil (or a camera) to record your observations. Be sure to have this field guide handy to help identify what you see. Identification is the first step toward understanding the natural world.

Rules for reptile watchers

- When you go exploring, take a buddy with you and tell a grown-up where you are going.
- Do not handle venomous reptiles! Keep a safe distance from them.
- If you move rocks or logs while searching for reptiles, carefully return them to their original position so that hiding places are preserved.
- Do not take home reptiles or amphibians. Enjoy them where you find them.
- Respect the natural world. Leave everything as you found it.

The Flattened Musk Turtle is the world's smallest turtle.

The world of reptiles

There are more than 6,800 reptile species in the world—and people are still discovering new ones. Just over 300 native species live in the United States and Canada: 2 crocodilians, 56 turtles, 1 worm lizard, 105 lizards, and 137 snakes. These animals come in many forms, ranging from sleek, whiplike snakes to huge, lumbering tortoises with heavy shells on their backs.

Turtle types

Turtles can be found on land and in water. Freshwater turtles, such as Painted Turtles, dwell in ponds and streams. Sea turtles, like the Leatherback, live in oceans and bays. Turtles of the tortoise family, such as the Desert Tortoise, stick to dry land.

MIDGETS TO MONSTERS

What does a two-inch lizard that can climb walls have in common with a 19-foot armored beast that looks like it's from the Age of Dinosaurs? They are both native North American reptiles.

At 2 inches long, the Reef Gecko (page 77) is North America's smallest reptile.

The American Alligator (page 50) is by far the largest reptile of North America. The record is 19 feet long!

Snake tales

Snakes are fascinating creatures that get along just fine without arms or legs. Some snakes can climb trees, many can swim, and others dig burrows. All are experts at finding and catching prey.

The Striped Racer (page 137) holds its head high as it searches for prey—which it captures in a burst of speed.

SPEEDSTERS

Everybody knows how slow tortoises are. But not all reptiles are such slow-pokes! Some reptiles are gone in a flash. Their names tell you that racerunners, whiptails, racers, and whipsnakes are the speedsters among North American lizards and snakes. They depend on quickness and agility to capture food and to outsmart enemies.

The Texas Spotted Whiptail (page 95) is one of the fastest reptiles.

Collared Lizard page 80

What is a reptile?

The first reptiles appeared on the earth about 300 million years ago. About 65 million years ago, many reptiles died off. Although more than 6,800 species survive today, only four main groups remain: crocodilians (alligators and crocodiles), turtles, tuatara (a lizardlike reptile from New Zealand), and squamata (lizards and snakes).

What do reptiles look like?

Reptiles come in all sizes and in a variety of unusual shapes. You may wonder what a turtle, a snake, a lizard, and an alligator have in common. The most obvious feature is a skin covering of dry, horny scales. The scales protect their bodies and help keep them from drying out. All reptiles carry their bodies low to the ground and, except for snakes and a few other types, have four limbs.

Painted Turtles (page 60) warming themselves in the sun

HOW DO REPTILES GET WARM?

Birds and mammals are warm-blooded and are able to keep their body temperature constant from the inside. But reptiles are cold-blooded, which means that their bodies warm up and cool down with the outside air temperature. They depend on an outside heat source—principally the sun—to keep them at temperatures that will permit activity and growth.

Reptile or amphibian?

Reptiles evolved from amphibians. But reptiles have adapted to life on land, while amphibians (salamanders and frogs) are very closely tied to water.

Some reptiles, like this Copperhead (page 146), give birth to live young rather than laying eggs.

Amphibians lay jelly-coated eggs that hatch in water. The young, called larvae, live in water and must go through a cycle of changes before they look like the adults.

Reptiles lay shelled eggs on land or bear their young alive on land. The hatchlings look like their parents.

JEFFERSON SALAMANDER (AMPHIBIAN)

No ear openings

Moist, naked skin

Clawless toes

NORTHERN ALLIGATOR LIZARD (REPTILE)

External ear openings (present in many reptiles)

Dry, scaly skin

Clawed toes

13

What's in a name?

Scientists like to put living things in groups based on their natural relationships. Reptiles are all in the animal kingdom and the reptile class, which has four orders: crocodilians, turtles, lizards and snakes, and tuatara. (This last order is not found in North America.) These orders are divided into families. Each family is further divided into genera (plural of *genus*), and genera are divided into species.

What is a species?

Reptiles that breed with each other and produce young are considered to be one species. Species members usually look like one another and look different from other species. When herpetologists study reptiles to determine what species they are, they look at things like patterns and colors, skeletal structure, and how the scales are arranged.

COMMON NAMES

Each reptile has a common name, and many reptiles have more than one. Reptiles are often given different common names in different places. The Eastern Hognose Snake is sometimes called the Puff Adder, Spreading Adder, Blow Viper, Spreadhead, or Sand Adder. To avoid confusion, herpetologists use the scientific name when talking about this snake.

Eastern Hognose Snake page 124

Two reptiles classified

The Desert Spiny Lizard and the Corn Snake belong to the animal kingdom and to the same phylum, class, and order. Here the similarity stops. They belong to different families, genera, and species.

Kingdom: Animalia
Phylum: Chordata
Class: Reptilia
Order: Squamata
Family: Colubridae
Genus: *Elaphe*
Species: *guttata*
(Corn Snake)

Kingdom: Animalia
Phylum: Chordata
Class: Reptilia
Order: Squamata
Family: Iguanidae
Genus: *Sceloporus*
Species: *magister*
(Desert Spiny Lizard)

Eastern Box Turtle page 58

SCIENTIFIC NAMES

Each reptile has a scientific name that is used around the world. A scientific name has two parts, the genus name and the species name. The Wood Turtle *(Clemmys insculpta)* and the Bog Turtle *(Clemmys muhlenbergii)* belong to the same genus *(Clemmys)*, which means that they are very closely related. The Eastern Box Turtle *(Terrapene carolina)* is in a different genus.

Wood Turtle page 57

Bog Turtle page 57

Subspecies and races

Some species of reptiles, such as the Milk Snake, look quite different in different regions. These different-looking reptiles of the same species are called subspecies or races. In the United States and Canada there are nine subspecies of Milk Snake.

Subspecies names

The scientific name of a subspecies has three parts. The first part is the genus, the second is the species, and the third is the subspecies. The scientific name of the Eastern Milk Snake is *Lampropeltis triangulum triangulum*, and that of the Scarlet Kingsnake is *Lampropeltis triangulum elapsoides*.

Eastern Milk Snake page 143

Believe it or not, these two different-looking snakes are the same species—the Milk Snake.

DIFFERENT— BUT ALIKE

One subspecies of Milk Snake, called the Eastern Milk Snake, is tan with brownish-red blotches, while another subspecies, called the Scarlet Kingsnake, has black, red, and yellow rings. These two subspecies of the Milk Snake look very different, but they can breed with each other and produce young.

Scarlet Kingsnake page 145

What do these two snakes have in common? They are both the same species: The Speckled Kingsnake is on the left, the California Kingsnake is on the right.

Reptile races

Many reptiles besides Milk Snakes look different in different areas and have many subspecies. Other examples are the Common Kingsnake, Eastern Racer, Eastern Rat Snake, Ringneck Snake, Coachwhip, Common Garter Snake, Western Whiptail Lizard, Fence Lizard, Diamondback Terrapin, Eastern Box Turtle, and Painted Turtle.

he southern subspecies of Painted urtle (below) has an orange stripe own its back. The western ubspecies of Painted Turtle (above) oes not have a back stripe.

Western Whiptail Lizard subspecies: California (above) and Great Basin (below)

17

Reptile anatomy

All reptiles are vertebrates, animals with backbones. Their bodies are covered with dry, horny scales or plates (called scutes). They are low to the ground, and all except snakes and a few lizards have four legs. Each of the main groups found in North America—alligators, turtles, lizards, and snakes—has its own unique characteristics.

TURTLE ANATOMY
Turtles and tortoises have scales on the head and the legs, but the rest of the body is encased in a rounded, bony shell. The upper portion of the shell, called the carapace, includes the spine and the ribs. It is joined to the lower part, the plastron, by a bridge of bone.

A turtle's top shell, shown here from the inside, includes the rib cage. Turtles are the only animals with their legs inside the rib cage.

Most turtles and tortoises can easily pull their heads straight back into their shells.

The bottom shell of some turtles, such as box turtles and Blanding's Turtle (left; page 61), is hinged and can be pulled up against the top shell (right), sealing the turtle safely inside.

The individual plates on a turtle's shell, like those on this Wood Turtle (page 57), are called scutes.

The bottom shell of the Painted Turtle (page 60), which is not hinged, can be quite colorful.

CROCODILIAN BODIES

Both the American Alligator and American Crocodile have torpedo-shaped bodies, well made for life in the water. They are keen-sighted and have sharp hearing. When they dive under, their nostrils close up and a clear membrane closes sideways across their eyes. A wide flap closes the rear of the throat so that they don't drown when they're pulling prey underwater.

Crocodilians have tough skin with large ridged scales.

The nostrils and eyes of crocodilians are perched on top of their heads, so they are able to see and breathe while almost entirely submerged.

LIZARDS

Lizards come in all shapes and sizes. Different species have developed special features to help them survive in different habitats. The Gila Monster has a stout body and beadlike scales and stores fat in its thick tail; it can survive without food for several months in its harsh desert environment. Some lizards, especially burrowing forms, have very small legs or no legs at all. Glass lizards are an example of legless lizards. They look like snakes but have movable eyelids, as do most lizards.

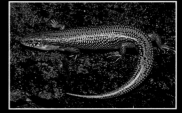

Skinks are recognized by their shiny, smooth, overlapping scales, short legs, and pointed snouts.

LIZARD SENSES

Most lizards see and hear well. They have external ear openings and their eyes have movable eyelids (unlike snakes).

The Collared Lizard (page 80) has the typical lizard shape (like a miniature dinosaur): big head, long tail, plump body covered with granular scales, and four feet with five clawed toes on each.

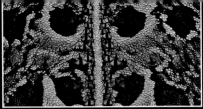

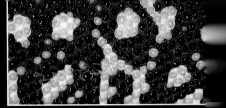

Texas Horned Lizard (page 89) scales and spines   *Gila Monster (page 98) beadlike scales*

SCALY SKIN

In some lizards the scales are small and grainlike, while in others they are large and platelike. The scales may be smooth or they may have little ridges called keels or they may even have developed into spines.

The "fringes" on the feet of fringe-toed lizards help them to walk on sand.

Some lizards have a "third eye," a tiny, light-sensitive, transparent structure on top of the head that helps them regulate how long they stay in the sun.

SNAKES

Snakes are marvels of nature. They have no eyelids, external ears, or legs, yet they live successfully without these body parts. Their slender shape means that the insides of their bodies are different from those of other vertebrates as well. In most snakes, the left lung is very tiny or absent and the left kidney is positioned behind the right one instead of side by side.

Snakes often shed their skin in one piece. After the skin on the snout splits, the skin peels off inside out as the snake moves forward.

SNAKE SKIN

Snakes shed the outer layer of their skin two or three times a year. This permits them to grow and also to discard the worn and damaged outer coat of skin. The old layer isn't shed until a new layer of skin has formed completely underneath it.

SNAKE EYES

Transparent eye caps protect the lidless eyes of snakes. Racers, whipsnakes, indigos, and some other species that are active during the day have excellent vision. Blind snakes can distinguish only light and dark.

Most nocturnal snakes, such as Copperheads, Night Snakes, and rattlesnakes, have vertical pupils that expand in low light.

Ringneck Snake (page 116) belly scales

Corn Snake (page 132) back scales

SNAKE SCALES

Snakes have large scales across the belly and smaller scales on the back. The back scales may have a smooth, polished appearance, or they may have a dull finish and a rough texture. The scales on water snakes have ridges, or keels, which help them move through water. Snakes that spend a lot of time burrowing have smooth scales, which enable them to move more easliy through the soil.

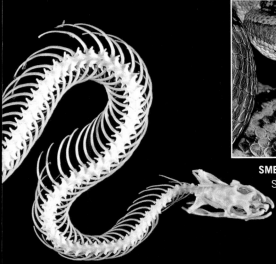
Snakes have an extremely long spine, with 200 to 400 vertebrae. (Humans have 32 to 34 vertebrae.) It takes a very complicated set of interconnected muscles to move all these bones.

SMELLING WITH FORKED TONGUE

Snakes cannot hear airborne sounds, but their other senses make up for that. By flicking their forked tongues they pick up chemicals left by other animals from the air or ground.

These chemicals are carried to an organ in the mouth that helps the snake figure out what (or whom) they came from. Guided by their tongues, snakes can trail food, follow one of their kind, or return to their shelter.

What do reptiles do all day?

What do reptiles do all day? Lots of things: bask in the sun to get their bodies moving, look for food, chase away rivals, escape from predators, lie in the shade, dig in the ground, and swim in the water.

This Chuckwalla (page 99) is basking on a rock to warm its body. When its temperature rises to a certain level, it will go look for food.

Communication

Like all animals, reptiles have developed many ways to communicate with one another. They use body signals and scent trails to get messages to others. With their eyes, ears, and tongues, they see and hear what is happening around them.

Warming up and cooling down

Reptiles spend a lot of time shuttling between warm and cool spots in their environment to regulate their body temperature. Most of the time when you see reptiles, they are basking, or lying in the sun to warm their bodies. To avoid overheating on hot summer days, they move into the shade, an underground retreat, or water to cool off. At night, snakes often gather on warm blacktop roads, and crocodilians and turtles may settle in water because it stays warm longer than air does.

LIZARD LINGO

Some geckos keep in touch by chirping and barking. Many members of the iguana group, such as the Collared Lizards, Chuckwallas, and anoles, signal others by bobbing their heads up and down vigorously.

One way the American Alligator (page 50) gets a message across is by opening its jaws and letting out a roar.

ALLIGATOR TALK

Alligators start communicating before they hatch! Young alligators chirp while still in the egg. These chirps tell their siblings that it's hatching time and signal their mother to dig open the nest and carry them to the water. During breeding season adult male alligators bellow loudly and slap their jaws on the water's surface to warn away rivals.

This Yellow Rat Snake (page 131) is gathering information with its forked tongue.

SNAKES DON'T TALK

Snakes and lizards flick out their tongues to smell, not to talk. But many snakes will hiss when they feel alarmed. Usually they'll make a hasty exit first!

When a male Green Anole (page 78) encounters another male, he pushes out his colorful throat fan, called a dewlap, and performs "push-ups."

Reproduction

All reptiles give birth on land. Most lay eggs, but a few bear live young. In reptiles, as in birds and mammals, the eggs are fertilized by the male while they are still in the body of the female. But before that can happen, a male and a female have to choose each other. This is called courting.

A male Desert Tortoise (left, page 69) courts a female by wagging his head at her.

TURTLE LOVE

Adult male turtles and tortoises court females in various ways. Male box turtles bite or head-butt females to win their favors. The male slider, which is much smaller than the female, flutters the long claws on his forelegs in front of the female's face in a kind of dance.

Hatchling turtles, like this Western Painted Turtle (page 61), are on their own from their first day.

TURTLE EGGS

Female turtles dig or scrape a nest in the ground, bury their eggs, and then leave them. Most sea turtles return to the beaches where they were born to lay their eggs. Some females may swim a thousand miles to their home beaches.

Newborn reptiles, like these rat snakes, have an "egg tooth" on the top of the snout that they use to slit open the eggshell.

GREAT BALLS OF SNAKES!

In areas where they are plentiful, many male garter or water snakes may court the same female, forming a "breeding ball" of intertwined bodies around her. Each male tries to be the one who gets to mate with her.

A female Red-sided Garter Snake (page 109) in a breeding ball

The female American Alligator (page 50) stays with her young for months to protect them from raccoons, birds, and other predators. This type of mothering behavior is very rare among reptiles.

MAMA GATORS

After laying her clutch of eggs, the female American Alligator covers them in a big mound of vegetation and earth. As the vegetation rots, it gives off heat, which keeps the eggs warm. The female gator remains nearby, and when she hears her young calling from inside the eggs, she digs open the nest, gathers up the young in her mouth, and carries them to the water.

Newborn Timber Rattlesnake page 148

LIZARD AND SNAKE BABIES

Most lizards and snakes lay eggs and leave the young to hatch and fend for themselves. Some lizards and snakes give birth to live young. This means that the young develop inside the body of the female, rather than in a laid egg. Garter snakes, water snakes, pit vipers (including rattlesnakes), and some spiny and horned lizards give birth this way.

27

Diet

Most reptiles eat a variety of foods, although a few species—such as the Striped Crayfish Snake, which eats only crayfish—specialize in one particular food. Many reptiles eat other animals, from insects and slugs to mammals like mice and rabbits. A small number of reptile species eat only plants.

LIZARD CHOW

A few lizards are plant-eaters (the Chuckwalla and Desert Iguana eat leaves and flowers of a desert plant called creosote bush), but most eat insects, spiders, snails, and other reptiles.

American Alligator (page 50) eating a raccoon

GATOR MEALS

American Alligators are the top meat-eaters in their habitats. Adults eat turtles, water birds, mammals, and occasionally smaller alligators. A large gator can take down a White-tailed Deer stopping for water.

The Desert Tortoise (page 69) is a plant-eater.

TURTLE FOOD

Tortoises eat plants, but most turtles eat both plants and animals. Freshwater turtles dine on insects, mollusks, crayfish, amphibian eggs and larvae, algae, and duckweed.

Collared Lizard (page 80) eating a fence lizard

SQUEEZE PLAY

Some snakes kill their prey by constricting, or squeezing it to death. Each time the victim breathes in, the snake winds itself tighter. Eventually the victim can't take another breath.

This Red Milk Snake (page 143) has wound its body around a Five-lined Skink (page 90). When the skink stops breathing, the snake will eat it.

These photographs show a Texas Coral Snake swallowing a Western Hook-nosed Snake (page 127).

The Corn Snake's (page 132) jaws expand so that it can swallow a mouse whole.

OPEN WIDE!

Chiefly meat-eaters, snakes dine on birds, insects, salamanders, frogs, lizards, snakes, eggs, and rodents. Snakes are able to open their jaws very wide in order to swallow their prey whole. Muscles along the snake's body push the victim along. It takes days for a snake to digest a large meal.

GONE FISHING

The Alligator Snapping Turtle fishes for meals, using a wormlike growth on its tongue. It lies in wait with its jaws wide open while wiggling the lure. Fish and other creatures that are attracted by the lure rarely escape the explosive jaw trap.

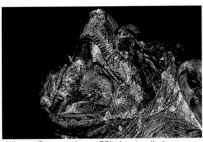

Alligator Snapper (page 53) showing its lure

Locomotion

Reptiles swim in the sea, climb trees and rocks, and burrow into the ground. Some reptiles are lightning fast, others are seriously slow. How do they all get around? In many wonderful ways.

LEGGY LIZARDS

Most lizards have four legs with five toes each. They walk in a symmetrical gait, moving both the front and the rear leg on one side at the same time.

Thousands of tiny hairlike hooks on each toe help geckos climb walls.

Tree-climbing species, such as anoles and some iguanas, have long slender legs, which help them in reaching from branch to branch and jumping between perches.

SLOW AND STEADY

Because they are encased in bony shells, tortoises are famously slow-moving. Their stout legs and short toes are built for life in the slow lane. North American tortoises move along at about a quarter of a mile an hour. Webbing between the toes of aquatic turtles allows them to move efficiently in water by swimming or walking along pond bottoms.

With its heavy shell on its back, the Three-Toed Box Turtle (page 59) walks slowly.

The front flippers of the Loggerhead (page 72) work like paddles, while the rear legs take care of steering.

SLITHERING SNAKES

Snakes evolved from lizards and lost their legs in the process, but at the same time they developed very efficient ways to move their bodies. They sometimes move in a series of S-shaped wavelike motions by pushing against the land or water with the sides of their curved bodies. Snakes do not move as fast as most people believe. The racer, one of the fastest, hits about four miles per hour.

The Sidewinder Rattlesnake crosses soft sand by sidewinding (moving diagonally in a series of parallel J-shaped curves).

BUILT TO MOVE

In spite of their huge size, alligators and crocodiles are fast swimmers. They swing their enormous tails to propel their torpedo-shaped bodies through the water.

American Alligator (page 50) swimming

Defense

Reptiles need to defend themselves against enemies, especially predators (animals that want to make a meal of them). They have many different ways of doing this: They race away, hide, blend into the background, puff up their bodies, and even play dead.

Eastern Hognose Snake (page 124) playing dead

Lizard tricks

Some kinds of lizards have tails that will break off when grabbed by an attacker. The lizard escapes, while the attacker is left with just the tail. Spiny lizards have sharp spines that discourage predators, and skinks have smooth overlapping scales that make them hard to hold onto.

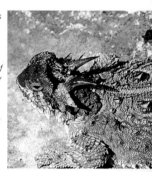

Horned lizards have special muscles that can burst tiny blood vessels at the edges of the eyes. They can squirt a stream of blood as far as 3 feet at an attacker.

Green Anole (page 78) with tail snapped off

Green Anole tail growing back

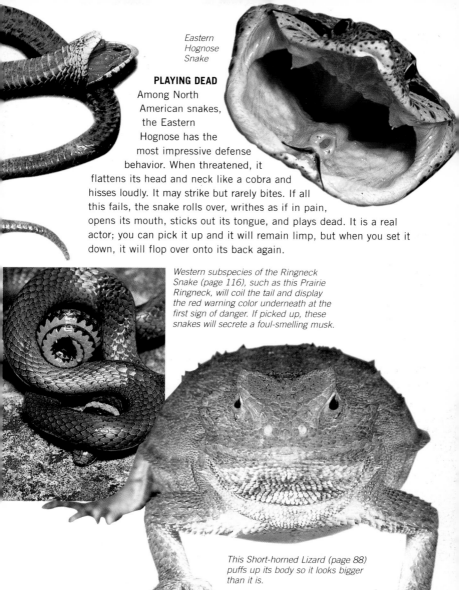

Eastern Hognose Snake

PLAYING DEAD

Among North American snakes, the Eastern Hognose has the most impressive defense behavior. When threatened, it flattens its head and neck like a cobra and hisses loudly. It may strike but rarely bites. If all this fails, the snake rolls over, writhes as if in pain, opens its mouth, sticks out its tongue, and plays dead. It is a real actor; you can pick it up and it will remain limp, but when you set it down, it will flop over onto its back again.

Western subspecies of the Ringneck Snake (page 116), such as this Prairie Ringneck, will coil the tail and display the red warning color underneath at the first sign of danger. If picked up, these snakes will secrete a foul-smelling musk.

This Short-horned Lizard (page 88) puffs up its body so it looks bigger than it is.

Camouflage clothing

Many lizards and snakes depend on camouflage (blending in with the background) to keep them safe from attackers. Fence lizards, for example, look like the bark of trees, especially when they remain perfectly still. Many desert reptiles are the color of sand. Anoles can change their skin color.

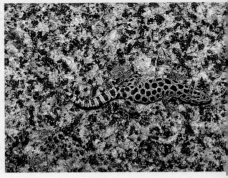

The Granite Night Lizard blends in with its rocky background.

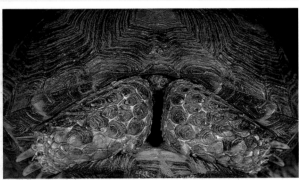

Texas Tortoise (page 69) tucked into its protective shell

Suits of armor

Some reptiles, such as alligators, are protected by their tough skins. Turtles and tortoises carry their defense system around with them—their shells. Box turtles have hinges in the bottom shell that enable them to pull it tightly against the top shell to completely protect their head and limbs from a fox or a raccoon. Some turtles, such as snapping, mud, and musk turtles, are colored to blend in with their habitat.

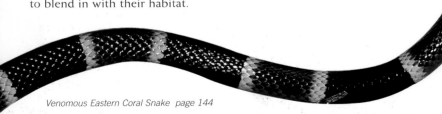

Venomous Eastern Coral Snake page 144

34

The Rough Green Snake (page 120) can be difficult to find in green vegetation.

The Mojave Fringe-toed Lizard buries itself in sand when it senses danger.

Copycats

Some harmless snakes have colors and patterns that are similar to those of venomous species. Any predator that fears the deadly Eastern Coral Snake is unlikely to attack the Scarlet Kingsnake, which is not venomous but looks quite similar to the coral snake.

American Alligator page 50

TOUGH SKINS

With their powerful jaws, sharp teeth, and thick hides, adult alligators and crocodiles have little to fear from predators, except humans. Female alligators protect their young from fish, birds, and other predators for months or even years.

Harmless Scarlet Kingsnake page 145

Beware: venomous reptiles

In the United States and Canada, only 21 species of snakes and one lizard are venomous, which means that they are able to pass venom into a victim through a bite.

The venomous species are the pit vipers (15 rattlesnakes, the Copperhead, and the Cottonmouth), three coral snakes, the Yellow-bellied Sea Snake (a rare visitor off southern California), and the Gila Monster. These species rarely bite people. Most bite only when harassed.

What is venom?

Venom is a brew of substances called enzymes, which can attack the blood, muscles, organs, and the central nervous system. Most venoms have more than one of these enzymes.

What's yellow and black and red all over? A coral snake. The snout is black at the tip and the red rings around the body are bordered by yellow on either side. The front fangs are short and fixed.

Eastern Coral Snake page 144

Copperhead (a pit viper) page 146

How can you identify a pit viper? Look for eyes with vertical pupils, a tiny pit in the face between the eye and the nostril, a spear-shaped head, long hinged fangs, and a stout body.

*Prairie Rattlesnake
(page 149) striking*

*Anyone foolish enough
to mess with a Gila
Monster (page 98) is
in for a very powerful
and painful bite.*

Warning!

Copperheads, Cottonmouths, and rattlesnakes are patterned to blend in with their surroundings. If a predator threatens, the rattlesnake will warn it away by vibrating its rattle, made up of horny segments at the tip of its tail. If all else fails, the snake will bite with its large fangs. Pit vipers are able to direct a strike in total darkness.

*Cottonmouth
page 147*

HOW TO AVOID VENOMOUS SNAKEBITE

Before you venture out, learn to recognize venomous species so that you can instantly identify them.

- Find out which venomous species live in your area and the habitats where you are likely to encounter them.

- Always go in the field with a friend and wear boots and loose-fitting pants.

- Watch where you place your hands and feet, especially when climbing or stepping over fences, large rocks, and logs.

- If you see (or hear) venomous reptiles, keep your distance. Do not go near them or try to touch them.

WHAT TO DO IF BITTEN

Venomous snakebites are rare, and they rarely kill humans. But if you are bitten by a venomous snake, you must go to a hospital and be treated. If bitten, move away from the snake and remain calm. Immobilize the bitten part, if possible, and go to a medical center. Do not "cut and suck" wounds, drink alcohol, or apply a tourniquet.

Rattlesnake

Where do reptiles live?

Field guides like this one tell you two things about where an animal lives: its range and its habitat. The range is the geographical area (such as the part of a country) where the animal lives. The habitat is the environment in which the animal lives. Deserts, woodlands, and marshes are habitats. A habitat contains the right combination of food, cover, and water a reptile needs to eat, sleep, hide from danger, and produce young.

HOME ON THE RANGE
Besides a geographical range a reptile has a home range, which is the patch, or collection of patches, of landscape an individual reptile uses during its life. A Spotted Turtle may spend its entire life within several acres of wetlands or move between a series of tiny wetlands half a mile apart. The marine-dwelling Green Turtle, on the other hand, may travel a thousand miles from its feeding grounds to its nesting beach.

EDGE HABITATS
The favorite haunt of many reptiles is where habitats merge. The weedy edge of a wetland, the thicket where field meets forest, or the spot where a rocky canyon stream breaks into a desert setting are prime locations to search for reptiles. These edge habitats are rich in species because they provide cover for more reptiles than neighboring environments do and attract species from both habitats.

Edge habitat reptiles: box turtles, skinks, fence lizards, alligator lizards, garter snakes, rattlesnakes, kingsnakes, milk snakes, rat snakes.

*Western Diamondback
page 149*

DESERTS AND BRUSHLANDS

Reptiles thrive in the sunny deserts and other dry areas of North America because they can so easily heat up their bodies, while their thick, scaly skin keeps them from drying out. Creosote bush desert, where creosote bush is the most common plant, is found in the Southwest. Sagebrush desert occurs in the high, cold Great Basin of Nevada, Utah, California, and Oregon. Brushlands are dry habitats with low shrubs and other woody plants. Chaparral is a habitat of low, dense, evergreen shrub thickets in the hot, dry, rolling hills of California and southern Oregon.

Desert and brushland reptiles:
Desert Tortoise, Chuckwalla,
Desert Iguana, horned lizards,
Gila Monster, Striped Whipsnake,
Long-nosed Snake, Night Snake,
Patch-nosed Snake, Western
Diamondback.

Chuckwalla page 99

GRASSLANDS

Many reptiles live in the sunny environs of meadows, fields, and prairies. Most of the fertile grasslands that once covered the Great Plains of central North America are gone, but patches of tall-grass prairie (rolling hills of waving 4- to 6-foot-tall grasses) remain in the Midwest, and short-grass prairies (large expanses of short grasses) are found in areas of low rainfall just east of the Rockies. Other grasslands include wet meadows (open wet fields where plants called tussock sedges, rushes, and blue flag are common), farm fields, and old fields (fields that were once farmed or logged and are slowly changing back to a woodland).

Grassland reptiles: Ornate Box Turtle, Six-lined
Racerunner, Lesser Earless Lizard, Great
Plains Skink, Smooth Green Snake,
Coachwhip, Massasauga,
Prairie Rattlesnake.

*Ornate Box Turtle
page 59*

FRESHWATER WETLANDS

Many reptiles spend part of their lives in or near water. They can be found around ponds, lakes, streams, rivers, and wetlands (land with standing water). Freshwater marshes are shallow-water wetlands with cattails, grasses, and similar plants, but no trees. Swamps are wetlands with trees. The cypress swamps of the Southeast are dominated by huge bald cypress trees. Bogs, formed by glaciers, are wetland pockets of acid water where sphagnum moss and heath plants thrive.

Freshwater reptiles: American Alligator, Painted Turtle, Northern and Southern water snakes, Eastern Ribbon Snake, Mud Snake.

*Eastern Ribbon Snake
page 107*

SALTWATER WETLANDS

Near coastlines, there are swamps, salt marshes, and waterways that are filled with a mix of salt and fresh water, called brackish water. Estuaries are areas where a freshwater river or stream meets the sea. Some southeastern wetlands have raised areas called hammocks that are high enough for trees growing on them to keep their roots above water and get oxygen.

Saltwater reptiles: Diamondback Terrapin, Loggerhead, Green Turtle, Hawksbill, Atlantic Ridley, Leatherback.

Loggerhead page 72

WHERE THE REPTILES ARE

In North America reptiles are most common in the warmer climates of the southern United States and least common in colder northern areas. The state of Florida has 2 crocodilians, 20 turtles, 18 lizards, and 42 native snakes, while Quebec province has no crocodilians or lizards, 7 turtles, and 7 snakes.

	UNITED STATES	CANADA
Crocodilians	2 species	0 species
Turtles	56 species	9 species
Lizards	105 species	5 species
Snakes	137 species	24 species

CITIES AND SUBURBS

Few reptiles live in very large cities, but a number of species may be found in small cities and towns that have preserved woodlands along watercourses or ravines and have interconnected parks.

City and suburb reptiles: Painted Turtle, anoles, skinks, fence lizards, Ringneck Snake, Brown Snake, Red-bellied Snake, Common Garter Snake, kingsnakes, rat snakes.

Mediterranean Gecko page 77

41

MOUNTAINS

Not many reptiles can survive at high altitudes. The cool environment makes it difficult for them to regulate their body temperature or find food or a safe place to spend the winter. The upper limit for most reptile species is 8,000 to 9,000 feet.

Mountain reptiles: Rubber Boa (to 10,000 feet), Western Diamondback (to 11,000 feet), Short-horned Lizard (to 11,300 feet), Spiny Lizard (over 12,000 feet), Western Terrestrial Garter Snake (to 13,000 feet).

Rubber Boa page 104

WOODLANDS

Woodlands provide shelter and food for reptiles and their prey—amphibians, birds, and small mammals. There are many types of woodlands in North America, from evergreen forests to hardwood forests, which are composed mainly of nonevergreens, such as oaks, maples, and beeches. In mixed forests, evergreens mingle with maples and beeches. Bottomland forests, found along river floodplains, are flooded each year by a foot or more of water. The great evergreen forests of the Northwest are dominated by pines, firs, spruces, and redwoods.

Northwestern forest reptiles: Northern Alligator Lizard, Short-horned Lizard, Western Fence Lizard, Western Skink, Rubber Boa, Western Terrestrial Garter Snake, Common Garter Snake, Ringneck Snake.

Western Terrestrial Garter Snake page 108

SOUTHWESTERN WOODLANDS

Woodlands of southwestern and central-western North America tend to be dryer and more open than the damp coastal forests of the Northwest. Rocky, sparsely timbered woodlands occur in the Southwest. Pinyon-juniper woodland is a dry habitat of pygmy pine and juniper trees between the Sierra Nevada and the Rocky Mountains.

Southwestern woodland reptiles: Fence Lizard, Tree Lizard, Northern Alligator Lizard, Western Whiptail, Short-horned Lizard, Ringneck Snake, Mountain Kingsnake, Western Terrestrial Garter Snake, Gopher Snake, Western Rattlesnake.

*Eastern Fence Lizard
page 82*

EASTERN WOODLANDS

In eastern North America, hardwood forests and mixed forests patchworked with fields and wetland pockets make a nice home for many reptiles. A forest of widely spaced pines covers much of the coastal plain of the Southeast. Forests composed of longleaf pine on southeastern flatlands are known as flatwoods. Dry, hilly, sandy areas of the Southeast, called sandhills, support an open woodland of turkey oak and longleaf pine with wiregrass covering the ground in between.

Eastern woodland reptiles: Eastern Box Turtle, Wood Turtle, Five-lined Skink, Ground Skink, Common Garter Snake, Rough Green Snake, Ringneck Snake, Copperhead, Timber Rattlesnake.

Eastern Box Turtle page 58

43

How to find reptiles

Y ou probably see birds every time you step outside. You may see squirrels or other small mammals when you go for a walk. Insects are buzzing around everywhere you go in the warmer months—even in your own bedroom! Reptiles, however, are shy and secretive creatures, and not many species are seen regularly.

Snakes are often found in hollow logs or under flat rocks or pieces of wood.

FLIPPING FOR REPTILES
Flipping over rocks, logs, and boards is one method for finding reptiles. You must take special care to return the objects that you've flipped to their original positions to maintain hiding spots.

STREET LIFE
During warm evenings, reptiles appear in car headlights as they rest on country roads, soaking up warmth from the blacktop. Some roads are well known to reptile watchers. You can often find species that are rarely seen at other times in such spots.

Reptiles, like this rattlesnake, often hide in piles of rubbish, under old boards, and in fallen-down buildings.

Viewing tips
- Look for reptiles in late spring, summer, and early fall, when the weather is warm enough for them to heat their bodies.
- Reptiles are most active on warm, sunny, windless days and warm evenings. They will sometimes come out of hiding after a heavy summer downpour or a warm evening shower.
- When looking for reptiles, try to keep the sun on your back, as basking reptiles will most likely be on the sunny side of a perch and you'll be able to see them better.
- Stop frequently to observe your surroundings. Use binoculars for scanning likely basking spots.

TO TOUCH OR NOT TO TOUCH?

Experienced reptile watchers may pick up a reptile when they see one. They know to handle the creature gently and to return it quickly to its retreat. If they want to study the reptile more, they take a photograph, make a drawing, or take notes. You should never touch a reptile unless you are certain of its identity. Do not attempt to capture venomous reptiles. Even nonvenomous reptiles can hurt you if they are teased or bothered!

If you pick up a reptile, like this kingsnake, be gentle, and put it back where you found it.

HOT SPOTS

Desert trails and the edges of woods and grasslands are good places to observe reptiles. Favorite basking sites include sunny areas with large rocks, stone walls, fence posts, tree trunks, and fallen timber. Mid-morning and late afternoon are the best times to look in hot areas, because most reptiles hide from the intense midday sun.

Lizards and snakes soak up the sun on rock walls.

Snappers and mud turtles are among the reptiles that live in freshwater marshes and swamps.

WET SPOTS

The edges of shallow weedy ponds, sluggish streams, marshes, and sheltered lake coves are favorite haunts of freshwater turtles and water, garter, and ribbon snakes. Look for basking sites such as sunlit banks, rocks, logs, and muskrat or beaver lodges.

Endangered species

Reptiles die when their habitats are destroyed. Lots of things can ruin a habitat: pollution, farming, logging, new roads and buildings, and mining. Many reptiles have been put in danger and more will come close to extinction if habitats are not saved.

The endangered Blunt-nosed Leopard Lizard, which lives in California's San Joaquin Valley, is severely threatened by agriculture and housing developments.

Why do we need reptiles?

Reptiles play a vital role in the web of life. Like birds, they eat countless rodents and insects and help control their numbers. They also are food for animals that are above them in the food chain. And lastly, they are fascinating creatures from which we can learn many things about our natural world and the history of life on earth.

ENDANGERED!
The American Crocodile may look as if it can take care of itself, but it has suffered from habitat loss. Today there are only about 500 of these crocs left in their native habitats in southern Florida.

TROUBLED TIMES FOR TURTLES

Freshwater turtles with tiny ranges cannot easily cope with pollution, changes to their environments, and being collected by pet sellers. Giant marine turtles fare no better than their tiny relatives. Hawksbill Turtles are killed for their shells, which are used for jewelry. Leatherbacks choke on castoff plastic bags, which they mistake for jellyfish. Loggerheads and Kemp's Ridley turtles drown in the nets of shrimp fishermen.

The Flattened Musk Turtle (pictured), found only in the Black Warrior River system of Alabama, and the Yellow-blotched Map Turtle, of the Pascagoula River system in Mississippi, are freshwater species that have become extremely rare.

GOPHER TORTOISES

Entire communities of animals depend on Gopher Tortoises. These turtles dig long burrows that are shared with more than 300 other kinds of animals, including Eastern Indigo Snakes and Eastern Diamondback Rattlers. Sadly, the tortoises' dry sand habitat is being destroyed by builders, who bulldoze the land and bury the tortoises. The tortoises are also killed for food by "gopher pullers," people who use long wire hooks to pull the tortoises from their burrows. During "rattlesnake roundups" gasoline is poured down the burrows to drive the rattlesnakes out, but many other species suffer as well.

Gopher Tortoise (page 68) at burrow entrance

The habitat of the endangered San Francisco Garter Snake, one of North America's most beautiful snakes, has been consumed by city growth.

Using the field guide

Yellow Rat Snake (page 131) eating frog

This section features 50 common North American reptiles and includes brief descriptions of 122 more. Color photographs and details about each reptile are included to help you identify it. Reptiles appearing on facing pages together are either related or share some traits or characteristics. When a subspecies appears as the main reptile on a page, the range map shows the geographical range of all the species' subspecies.

ICONS

These icons appear on each left-hand page in the field guide. They identify a reptile's general shape and category.

Crocodilians

Turtles

Lizards

Snakes

REPTILE I.D. TIPS

- Sometimes a single field mark, like a spot behind th͏e eye, is more important in identifying a species than more complete description. The animal's color, for instance, may vary so much that it is not important.
- Stripes are lines that follow the reptile's length (in the same direction as the backbone). Bands or rings circle around the body, like a belt.
- Blotches are bigger than spots and often odd-shaped. Saddles are blotches on the back or tail that extend down onto the sides, like a saddle on a horse.

American Alligator page 50

SHAPE ICON

This icon identifies the featured reptile's general shape and category.

NAME

Each reptile's common and scientific names appear here.

BOX HEADING

The box heading alerts you to other reptiles covered in the box that are similar in some way to the main reptile on the page.

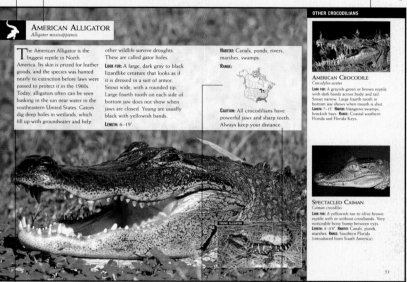

OTHER CROCODILIANS

AMERICAN ALLIGATOR
Alligator mississippiensis

The American Alligator is the biggest reptile in North America. Its skin is prized for leather goods, and the species was hunted nearly to extinction before laws were passed to protect it in the 1960s. Today, alligators often can be seen basking in the sun near water in the southeastern United States. Gators dig deep holes in wetlands, which fill up with groundwater and help other wildlife survive droughts. These are called gator holes.

LOOK FOR: A large, dark gray to black lizardlike creature that looks as if it is dressed in a suit of armor. Snout wide, with a rounded tip. Large fourth tooth on each side of bottom jaw does not show when jaws are closed. Young are usually black with yellowish bands.

LENGTH: 6–19'.

HABITAT: Canals, ponds, rivers, marshes, swamps.

RANGE:

CAUTION: All crocodilians have powerful jaws and sharp teeth. Always keep your distance.

YOUNG ALLIGATOR

AMERICAN CROCODILE
Crocodylus acutus

LOOK FOR: A grayish-green or brown reptile with dark bands across body and tail. Snout narrow. Large fourth tooth in bottom jaw shows when mouth is shut. **LENGTH:** 7–15'. **HABITAT:** Mangrove swamps, brackish bays. **RANGE:** Coastal southern Florida and Florida Keys.

SPECTACLED CAIMAN
Caiman crocodilus

LOOK FOR: A yellowish-tan to olive-brown reptile with or without crossbands. Very noticeable bony bump between eyes. **LENGTH:** 4–8'8". **HABITAT:** Canals, ponds, marshes. **RANGE:** Southern Florida (introduced from South America).

51

IDENTIFICATION CAPSULE

The identification capsule covers all the details you need to identify a reptile: color, pattern, size, shape, and other field marks discussed in this book.

RANGE AND HABITAT

The range and habitat listings tell you at a glance whether or not a reptile is likely to be seen in your area.

CAUTION

A caution listing alerts you to reptiles that may be dangerous.

AMERICAN ALLIGATOR
Alligator mississippiensis

The American Alligator is the biggest reptile in North America. Its skin is prized for leather goods, and the species was hunted nearly to extinction before laws were passed to protect it in the 1960s. Today, alligators often can be seen basking in the sun near water in the southeastern United States. Gators dig deep holes in wetlands, which fill up with groundwater and help other wildlife survive droughts. These are called gator holes.

LOOK FOR: A large, dark gray to black lizardlike creature that looks as if it is dressed in a suit of armor. Snout wide, with a rounded tip. Large fourth tooth on each side of bottom jaw does not show when jaws are closed. Young are usually black with yellowish bands.

LENGTH: 6–19'.

HABITAT: Canals, ponds, rivers, marshes, swamps.

RANGE:

CAUTION: All crocodilians have powerful jaws and sharp teeth. Always keep your distance.

AMERICAN CROCODILE
Crocodylus acutus

LOOK FOR: A grayish-green or brown reptile with dark bands across body and tail. Snout narrow. Large fourth tooth in bottom jaw shows when mouth is shut. **LENGTH:** 7–15'. **HABITAT:** Mangrove swamps, brackish bays. **RANGE:** Coastal southern Florida and Florida Keys.

SPECTACLED CAIMAN
Caiman crocodilus

LOOK FOR: A yellowish-tan to olive-brown reptile with or without crossbands. Very noticeable bony bump between eyes. **LENGTH:** 4'–8'8". **HABITAT:** Canals, ponds, marshes. **RANGE:** Southern Florida (introduced from South America).

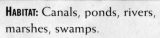

YOUNG ALLIGATOR

SNAPPING TURTLE
Chelydra serpentina

ALLIGATOR SNAPPING TURTLE
Macroclemys temminckii

LOOK FOR: A very large freshwater turtle (largest in U.S. and Canada) with 3 high keels on shell and a huge head with a hooked beak. Shell and skin dark brown to grayish. **LENGTH:** 13–30". **HABITAT:** Deep rivers, lakes. **RANGE:** Mississippi Valley, eastern Texas to Florida, rivers draining into Gulf of Mexico.

The Snapper is the largest turtle in most of its range. It is nearly always in water, hiding in the muck in shallows, under stumps in deep pools, or in old muskrat lodges. Females can be seen on land in June moving to sunny nesting spots. Snappers have huge appetites. They eat insects, fish, frogs, snakes, birds, muskrats, and many kinds of plants.

LOOK FOR: A large tan, brown, or gray turtle with a big head and strong jaws. Very long tail has sawtoothlike scales along the top.

LENGTH: 8–20".

HABITAT: All freshwater habitats; coastal marshes.

RANGE:

CAUTION: When approached in water Snappers usually rush for cover, but on land they can be very aggressive if bothered—and can bite savagely.

STINKPOT
Sternotherus odoratus

The Stinkpot, or Common Musk Turtle, likes muddy-bottomed, shallow waters. It walks along the bottom, looking for worms, snails, crayfish, and tadpoles. When resting it may look like an algae-covered stone. Its neck is so long that it can reach its back legs.

LOOK FOR: A small, short-tailed, gray or brown turtle with 2 whitish stripes on each side of its head and fleshy bumps on its chin and throat. Small bottom shell has 1 hinge (not always evident).

LENGTH: 2–5".

HABITAT: Slow rivers, streams, ponds, swamps, canals.

LOGGERHEAD MUSK TURTLE
Sternotherus minor

LOOK FOR: A brown turtle with 3 keels on upper shell and 1 hinge on lower shell.
LENGTH: 3–5". **HABITAT:** Streams, rivers, lakes.
RANGE: Southeastern U.S.

EASTERN MUD TURTLE
Kinosternon subrubrum

LOOK FOR: A turtle with a smooth brown upper shell, and a large lower shell with 2 hinges. **LENGTH:** 3–4½". **HABITAT:** Shallow, mud-bottomed waters. **RANGE:** Eastern U.S.

YELLOW MUD TURTLE
Kinosternon flavescens

LOOK FOR: A turtle with a smooth brown upper shell and a yellowish throat. Lower shell yellow with 2 hinges. **LENGTH:** 4–6". **HABITAT:** Quiet waters. **RANGE:** Central and southwestern U.S.

RANGE:

CAUTION: When picked up, Stinkpots often leak a foul-smelling liquid called musk and may try to bite.

55

SPOTTED TURTLE
Clemmys guttata

Spring is the best time to see this cool-weather turtle. "Spotties" bask early in the day, then search the shallows for water insects, snails, and frog eggs. In summer they hide on land and wait for fall rains before moving back to water. They spend the winter in groups in old muskrat tunnels.

Spotties and their relatives, shown at right, are all declining in number and need to be protected. Don't take them home!

LOOK FOR: A small black turtle with a variable number of round yellow spots on upper shell.

LENGTH: 3½–5".

HABITAT: Marshes, woodland streams, swamps, and bogs.

RANGE:

WOOD TURTLE
Clemmys insculpta

LOOK FOR: A turtle with a sculptured shell and yellow or orange under the neck and legs. **LENGTH:** 5½–9". **HABITAT:** Streams and nearby fields and woodlands. **RANGE:** Northeastern U.S. and Great Lakes region.

BOG TURTLE
Clemmys muhlenbergii

LOOK FOR: A dark brown turtle with a large orange blotch on each side of head. **LENGTH:** 3–4". **HABITAT:** Wet meadows, bogs. **RANGE:** Eastern U.S. (scattered throughout).

WESTERN POND TURTLE
Clemmys marmorata

LOOK FOR: A turtle with a yellow lower shell; black flecks on leg scales. **LENGTH:** 3½–7½". **HABITAT:** Streams, rivers, ditches. **RANGE:** West Coast of U.S. and British Columbia.

EASTERN BOX TURTLE
Terrapene carolina carolina

A warm-weather shower often coaxes box turtles out of their hiding spots to drink and find worms or slugs to eat. They also like mushrooms and fruits. During hot summer periods, box turtles may seek swampy pools and stay there for days, half-buried in the mud. Box turtles pass the winter on land under leaves and other woodland debris.

Look for: A land-dwelling turtle with a highly domed, colorful upper shell and a hinged lower shell that allows the shell to close tightly.

THREE-TOED BOX TURTLE
Terrapene carolina triunguis

LOOK FOR: A box turtle with a plain or faintly patterned, dark brown to reddish-brown shell. Orange on head. Three toes on back foot. **LENGTH:** 4½–7". **HABITAT:** Woodlands; nearby grasslands. **RANGE:** South-central U.S.

FLORIDA BOX TURTLE
Terrapene carolina bauri

LOOK FOR: A box turtle with a pattern of lines on dark brown upper shell and 2 stripes on head. **LENGTH:** 5–7½". **HABITAT:** Pine flatwoods and damp hammocks. **RANGE:** Florida.

ORNATE BOX TURTLE
Terrapene ornata

LOOK FOR: A box turtle with a pattern of yellow lines on upper and lower shells. **LENGTH:** 4–6". **HABITAT:** Prairies. **RANGE:** Central and southwestern U.S.

LENGTH: 4½–7½".

HABITAT: Woodlands, old fields, wet meadows.

RANGE:

EASTERN PAINTED TURTLE
Chrysemys picta picta

One of the most abundant turtles across its range, the colorful Painted Turtle can be seen basking in the morning and in late afternoon on a favorite log. Sometimes many of them are stacked upon one another. Occasionally, Painted Turtles are seen in winter, moving about under the ice of a frozen pond.

LOOK FOR: A small turtle with a very smooth, olive to black upper shell with red marks along edge. Lower shell unhinged.

LENGTH: 4–9½".

HABITAT: Marshes, ponds, lake shallows, slow creeks.

RANGE:

WESTERN PAINTED TURTLE
Chrysemys picta bellii
LOOK FOR: A Painted Turtle with a very colorful pattern on lower shell. **LENGTH:** 4–10".
HABITAT: Slow streams, ponds, lakes, marshes.
RANGE: Western half of Painted Turtle's range.

CHICKEN TURTLE
Deirochelys reticularia
LOOK FOR: A turtle with a long striped neck and pattern of fine lines on tan to olive shell. **LENGTH:** 4–10". **HABITAT:** Weedy ponds, marshes, cypress swamps. **RANGE:** Southeastern U.S.

BLANDING'S TURTLE
Emydoidea blandingii
LOOK FOR: A turtle with a yellow neck, speckled shell, and hinged lower shell.
LENGTH: 5–10". **HABITAT:** Shallow lakes, ponds, marshes. **RANGE:** Great Lakes region; scattered in Northeast.

61

COMMON MAP TURTLE
Graptemys geographica

If you want to see map turtles, you'll have to sneak up on them: They disappear into the water at the slightest disturbance. Look for them with binoculars at midday, basking on logs and rocks offshore near deep water. Females have large heads with very strong jaws for breaking snail shells. There are 12 species of map turtles.

LOOK FOR: A medium-size turtle with a maplike pattern on its olive-green shell and a triangular mark behind its eye. In youngsters, a low ridge with short spines runs down middle of upper shell.

FALSE MAP TURTLE
Graptemys pseudogeographica

LOOK FOR: An olive-green turtle with either 4–7 neck stripes that touch edge of eye or a long curved bar behind eye with white iris and round pupil. **LENGTH:** Female 5–10½"; male 3½–5½". **HABITAT:** Rivers, lakes. **RANGE:** Missouri and Mississippi rivers to Gulf of Mexico.

OUACHITA MAP TURTLE
Graptemys ouachitensis

LOOK FOR: An olive-green to brown turtle with a square, rectangular, or oval mark behind eye and 1–9 neck stripes reaching eye. **LENGTH:** Female 5–9½"; male 3½–5½". **HABITAT:** Swift rivers, lakes, swamps. **RANGE:** Minnesota and Wisconsin to Louisiana.

ALABAMA MAP TURTLE
Graptemys pulchra

LOOK FOR: A turtle with a masklike head pattern and a black line down center of upper shell. **LENGTH:** Female 7–10½"; male 3–5". **HABITAT:** Swift streams and rivers with log snags. **RANGE:** Mobile Bay watershed of Alabama and Georgia.

LENGTH: Female 7–10½"; male 3½–6".
HABITAT: Lakes and rivers.
RANGE:

NORTHERN DIAMONDBACK TERRAPIN
Malaclemys terrapin terrapin

This strong-jawed turtle is well suited for eating periwinkles, mussels, and crabs. In the past, it was heavily used in soups because of its sweet meat. Today terrapins are threatened by pollution and coastal development. They often drown in pots people set out to catch crabs.

LOOK FOR: A small turtle in coastal waters with ringlike grooves and ridges on the scutes of its upper shell. Its skin is light-colored with dark markings.

LENGTH: Female 6–9"; male 4–5½".

MISSISSIPPI DIAMONDBACK TERRAPIN
Malaclemys terrapin pileata

LOOK FOR: A terrapin with black knobs down center of back and an upturned, orange-edged shell. **LENGTH:** Female 6–8"; male 4–5½". **HABITAT:** Coastal marshes. **RANGE:** Florida panhandle to western Louisiana.

ORNATE DIAMONDBACK TERRAPIN
Malaclemys terrapin macrospilota

LOOK FOR: A terrapin with yellow-orange spots in the centers of its scutes. **LENGTH:** Female 6–8"; male 4–5½". **HABITAT:** Brackish streams with mangrove trees. **RANGE:** West coast of Florida.

RED-EARED SLIDER
Trachemys scripta elegans

Sliders are the most variable of all turtles, with more than a dozen known races, including the familiar Red-eared Slider. Millions of slider hatchlings raised on turtle farms are sold as pets each year around the world. A few sliders have lived 40 years in captivity. The slider's diet changes with age. It starts out eating insects, shifting to plants as it matures.

LOOK FOR: A medium to large freshwater turtle with a large red stripe behind each eye. The oval shell is green with yellow and black bars. The yellow lower shell has a single black mark in each scute. Males have large, curved front claws.

YELLOW-BELLIED SLIDER
Trachemys scripta scripta

LOOK FOR: A slider with a large yellow blotch behind eye and a pair of black blotches at front of lower shell. **LENGTH:** 5–11". **HABITAT:** Weedy ponds, lakes, ditches, rivers. **RANGE:** Southeastern U.S.

RED-BELLIED TURTLE
Pseudemys rubriventris

LOOK FOR: A big basking turtle with a reddish lower shell. **LENGTH:** 10–15". **HABITAT:** Deep ponds, lakes, rivers. **RANGE:** Mid-Atlantic coast states.

RIVER COOTER
Pseudemys concinna

LOOK FOR: A large turtle with yellow head stripes, lower shell yellow or patterned. **LENGTH:** 9–15½". **HABITAT:** Slow streams with basking sites. **RANGE:** Southern U.S.

LENGTH: 5–11".

HABITAT: Quiet waters with lots of plants and basking logs.

RANGE:

GOPHER TORTOISE
Gopherus polyphemus

True to its name, the Gopher Tortoise is a champion digger. Its burrow may be more than 40 feet long. The burrow serves as a shelter from the summer sun, winter chill, and predators. Many other creatures, including Eastern Indigo Snakes and Eastern Diamondback Rattlesnakes, may share this tortoise's burrow. Gopher Tortoises eat leaves, flowers, and fruits.

LOOK FOR: Burrows and mounds of sand. A large, dark, heavy-shelled land turtle with shovellike front feet and rear legs shaped like those of elephants. Its head is large and rounded.

LENGTH: 6–15".

HABITAT: Sandhills, pine flatwoods, beach scrub.

RANGE:

TEXAS TORTOISE
Gopherus berlandieri

LOOK FOR: A small brown tortoise with yellowish centers in scutes on upper shell. Wedge-shaped head comes to point at snout. **LENGTH:** 5½–9". **HABITAT:** Open scrub woods. **RANGE:** Southern Texas.

DESERT TORTOISE
Gopherus agassizii

LOOK FOR: A large tortoise with a tan to black shell with orangish centers in scutes. Head rounded. **LENGTH:** 8½–14". **HABITAT:** Deserts, dry rocky hillsides, canyon bottoms. **RANGE:** Arizona, Nevada, southern California.

69

SPINY SOFTSHELL
Apalone spinifera

Softshells are easy to identify by their shells, which are covered with skin instead of horny plates. Spiny Softshells bask on sandbars or banks close to water and can escape with dazzling speed. They are great swimmers and cruise the shallows for prey or lie buried in the soft bottom with only the head exposed, waiting for food.

LOOK FOR: A flattened, olive-green to tan turtle with a pancakelike, round, leathery shell with small spines on the front edge.

LENGTH: Female 7–21"; male 5–9".

HABITAT: Soft-bottomed waters, rivers, marshy creeks, reservoirs.

RANGE:

SMOOTH SOFTSHELL
Apalone mutica

LOOK FOR: An olive-green to orange-brown softshell turtle with a very smooth shell. **LENGTH:** Female 6½–14"; male 4½– 7". **HABITAT:** Large rivers, streams, lakes. **RANGE:** Central and southeastern U.S.

FLORIDA SOFTSHELL
Apalone ferox

LOOK FOR: A dark brown to brownish-gray softshell turtle with bumps on the front edge of its shell. **LENGTH:** Female 11–24"; male 6–12". **HABITAT:** Marshes, swamps, canals, rivers. **RANGE:** Southeastern U.S.

LOGGERHEAD
Caretta caretta

Female Loggerheads come ashore at night in summer and dig their nests above the high-water mark in front of dunes. They may lay as many as five clutches, each with about 100 eggs, during a season. Sadly, this magnificent turtle is a threatened species. Its nesting habitats are being destroyed by coastal development, and large numbers of Loggerheads drown in fishing nets each year.

LOOK FOR: A medium to large sea turtle with a large head, blunt jaws, a reddish-brown shell, and paddlelike front legs.

LENGTH: 31–48".

HABITAT: Coastal bays, salt marshes, river mouths. Nests on beaches.

RANGE:

ATLANTIC RIDLEY
Lepidochelys kempii

LOOK FOR: A sea turtle with a round grayish-green shell. **LENGTH:** 23–29". **HABITAT:** Shallow coastal waters. **RANGE:** Gulf of Mexico; juveniles along Atlantic Coast.

GREEN TURTLE
Chelonia mydas

LOOK FOR: A sea turtle with a wide, oval, brown shell with no keels. **LENGTH:** 28–60". **HABITAT:** Open seas, sea-grass pastures. **RANGE:** Warm waters of Atlantic and Pacific oceans.

HAWKSBILL
Eretmochelys imbricata

LOOK FOR: A sea turtle with a hawklike beak. Brown shell with yellow pattern, central keel, and overlapping scutes. Yellow skin between head scales. **LENGTH:** 30–36". **HABITAT:** Open seas, reefs, bays. **RANGE:** Atlantic and Pacific oceans.

73

LEATHERBACK TURTLE
Dermochelys coriacea

The Leatherback is the world's largest turtle. It is a strong swimmer that travels long distances from tropical to temperate waters, following drifting schools of jellyfish, its main food. Spines inside its mouth and throat help the turtle swallow its slippery meals. Leatherbacks are sometimes seen in large groups. They can dive to depths greater than 3,000 feet.

Look for: A giant dark gray to bluish-black sea turtle with 7 ridges running down the top of its shell. The shell is covered with smooth skin instead of the hard plates seen in other sea turtles. Its paddlelike flippers lack claws.

Length: 4'6"–8'.

Habitat: Open ocean, bays.

Range:

WESTERN BANDED GECKO
Coleonyx variegatus

By day the Western Banded Gecko hides in rocky crevices or under plant litter or boards. At night it leaves its retreat in search of insects and spiders. Most often, Western Banded Geckos are seen at night, looking like pale stick figures crossing back roads. When startled, these geckos may run with their tails curled over their backs. They sometimes squeak when picked up.

LOOK FOR: A soft-skinned lizard with dark bands that may be broken up into spots. Large eyes with vertical pupils and moveable eyelids.

LENGTH: 4–6".

HABITAT: Deserts, rocky areas.

RANGE:

MEDITERRANEAN GECKO
Hemidactylus turcicus

LOOK FOR: A pale-skinned lizard with big eyes and wide toe pads. Active at night; often seen on walls near lights where insects gather. **LENGTH:** 4–5". **HABITAT:** Urban areas, buildings, tree crevices. **RANGE:** Scattered across Deep South.

REEF GECKO
Sphaerodactylus notatus

LOOK FOR: A small lizard with speckled dark brown skin. Two white spots on neck of female. No eyelids. **LENGTH:** 2–2½". **HABITAT:** Gardens, damp woods. **RANGE:** Tip of Florida and Florida Keys.

DESERT NIGHT LIZARD
Xantusia vigilis

LOOK FOR: A lizard with velvety skin, usually with dark spots. Large square belly scales. Vertical pupils; no eyelids. **LENGTH:** 3½–5". **HABITAT:** Dry lands in rock crevices or under plant debris. **RANGE:** Southwestern U.S.

77

GREEN ANOLE
Anolis carolinensis

The Green Anole is sometimes incorrectly called a chameleon. Like chameleons, anoles are color-change artists. Their skin color depends on body temperature, environment, and mood. When a male is approached by a rival anole, he raises a crest on his neck and turns emerald green with a black patch behind the eye. He bobs his head up and down at the intruder and extends his throat fan. Sometimes rivals chase each other high in trees. Female anoles lay one egg at a time throughout the spring and summer.

LOOK FOR: A green to brown lizard with a pink fan-shaped flap of skin on throat. Can quickly change color from green to spotted green and brown to all brown.

LENGTH: 5–9".

HABITAT: Parks, woods, old buildings, and lots, palm fronds, thickets.

RANGE:

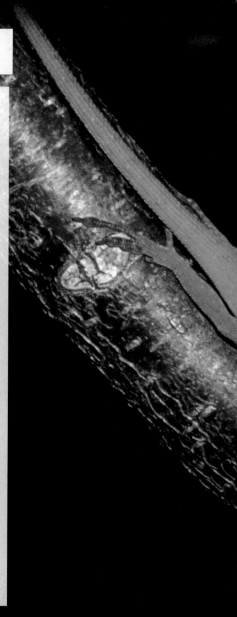

SHEDDING SKIN

BROWN ANOLE
Anolis sagrei

LOOK FOR: An anole with brown skin and white-fringed, orange-red throat fan. **LENGTH:** 5–8". **HABITAT:** Common around buildings and trash heaps. **RANGE:** Introduced to Florida and southern Texas.

COLLARED LIZARD
Crotaphytus collaris

The Collared Lizard is a well-designed predator. After sunning on a favorite lookout spot, it will jump nimbly from rock to rock, chasing down large insects, spiders, other lizards, and small snakes. It is hard to sneak up on a Collared Lizard; when alarmed, the animal quickly finds an escape burrow.

LOOK FOR: A long-tailed lizard with an oversize head and 2 black collars across back of neck. Color varies: may be yellow, greenish, brownish, or bluish with light spots. Runs on its hind legs and looks like a miniature *Tyrannosaurus rex* dinosaur.

LENGTH: 8–14".

LONG-NOSED LEOPARD LIZARD
Gambelia wislizenii

Look for: A large, long-tailed, gray, brown, or pinkish lizard with dark spots and light crossbars. **Length:** 8½–15". **Habitat:** Dry grasslands and deserts with scattered low bushes. **Range:** Western U.S. from Oregon and Idaho to California and Texas.

DESERT IGUANA
Dipsosaurus dorsalis

Look for: A large, long-tailed, pale gray lizard with brown bars on sides. Small head and short snout. Row of raised scales down back forms a low ridge. **Length:** 10–16". **Habitat:** Creosote bush deserts, sandy plains. **Range:** Southwestern U.S.

Habitat: Limestone ledges, dry rocky hillsides, gullies, canyons.

Range:

Caution: Watch out! These lizards bite hard when caught.

81

EASTERN FENCE LIZARD
Sceloporus undulatus

This spiny-scaled lizard is fond of bright, sunny habitats, where it basks on wood fences, tree stumps, and rocks. If you get too close, this lizard will dart to the opposite side of a nearby tree, and if you try to follow, will circle higher and higher. The Eastern Fence Lizard is a member of a genus, called spiny lizards, with 16 species in the United States.

LOOK FOR: A lizard with a backward pointing spine on each of the scales on its back. Males have blue patches on the sides of the throat and sides of the belly.

LENGTH: 4–7½".

HABITAT: Open pine woods, grassy dunes, brushlands, prairies, rocky hillsides, abandoned buildings.

WESTERN FENCE LIZARD
Sceloporus occidentalis

LOOK FOR: A spiny lizard with yellow or orange on rear of legs; males have blue on middle of throat and sides of belly. **LENGTH:** 6–9". **HABITAT:** Grasslands, open forests, farms. **RANGE:** Far western U.S.

DESERT SPINY LIZARD
Sceloporus magister

LOOK FOR: A light-colored spiny lizard with large pointed scales and a black triangle-shaped mark on side of neck. **LENGTH:** 7–12". **HABITAT:** Deserts, grasslands, dry woodlands. **RANGE:** Western Texas to southern California.

SAGEBRUSH LIZARD
Sceloporus graciosus

LOOK FOR: A spiny lizard with black bar on shoulder and rusty patch on front leg. **LENGTH:** 4½–6". **HABITAT:** Sagebrush deserts, juniper-pine woodlands, redwood forests. **RANGE:** Western U.S.

RANGE:

83

SIDE-BLOTCHED LIZARD
Uta stansburiana

The Side-blotched Lizard is one of the most commonly seen lizards in its dry western habitats. It lives on the ground and seldom climbs very high. After basking in the sun, these lizards dine on insects and spiders, all the while trying to keep an eye out for predatory lizards, snakes, and birds that might eat them.

LOOK FOR: A small brownish lizard with a black spot behind its front leg and a fold of skin across its throat.

LENGTH: 4–6".

TREE LIZARD
Urosaurus ornatus

LOOK FOR: A brownish-gray lizard with 2 rows of large scales down center of back and skin fold across throat. Male has patches of blue on belly. **LENGTH:** 4½–6".
HABITAT: River-edge woodlands, deserts to evergreen forests. **RANGE:** Western U.S. from southern Wyoming to southeastern California and central Texas.

BANDED ROCK LIZARD
Petrosaurus mearnsi

LOOK FOR: A flat-bodied lizard with a black ring around neck and dark and light bands around tail. **LENGTH:** 8½–11". **HABITAT:** Narrow, shady canyons with large rocks. **RANGE:** Southern California.

LESSER EARLESS LIZARD
Holbrookia maculata

Earless lizards are well suited for life on and below sand. They have no ear openings to get plugged up with sand, and their heads push easily into the sand for burrowing. They bask early in the morning and begin to forage for grasshoppers, wasps, and beetles when their body temperature reaches about 95°F. When the soil temperature reaches 104°F, the lizards disappear underground. They reappear in late afternoon after the temperature has fallen and bask in the sun again.

LOOK FOR: A small gray to brown lizard with two black spots behind front leg. No ear openings; no black bars on underside of tail.

LENGTH: 4–5".

HABITAT: Prairies, deserts, sand dunes, dry woodlands, farms.

RANGE:

GREATER EARLESS LIZARD
Cophosaurus texanus
LOOK FOR: An earless lizard with 2 curved black bars in front of each hind leg and black bars on underside of tail. **LENGTH:** 3–7". **HABITAT:** Rocky hillsides, deserts with scattered plants. **RANGE:** Central Texas to central Arizona.

ZEBRA-TAILED LIZARD
Callisaurus draconoides
LOOK FOR: An eared lizard with black bars on tail; males have 2 black bars on side that run into blue patches on belly. **LENGTH:** 6–9".
HABITAT: Open deserts. **RANGE:** Nevada, Arizona, southern California.

COLORADO DESERT FRINGE-TOED LIZARD
Uma notata
LOOK FOR: An eared lizard with bristlelike fringe on toes and a black spot in an orange stripe on side of belly. **LENGTH:** 5–7".
HABITAT: Dunes, deserts, and sandy riverbanks. **RANGE:** Southwestern U.S.

SHORT-HORNED LIZARD
Phrynosoma douglasii

The seven species of horned lizards in the United States are often called horned toads, because of their wide, flattened bodies and prominent armor of sharp-pointed horns on their heads. They are ground-dwellers and are usually found basking in dry, sandy environments. The Short-horned Lizard, an ant eater, may be found from desert flats to pine forest clearings above 10,000 feet. If disturbed, these lizards may squirt blood from their eyelids.

Look for: A flat-bodied gray, yellowish, or reddish-brown lizard with a crown of short, stubby horns on head; deep indent in center of crown. Row of pointed, bristly scales along each side of body.

LENGTH: 2½–6".

HABITAT: Shortgrass prairies, sagebrush deserts, dry, open woodlands, mountain meadows, prairie-dog towns.

RANGE:

DESERT HORNED LIZARD
Phrynosoma platyrhinos

LOOK FOR: A reddish to tan to dark gray horned lizard with a short crown of horns; row of pointed scales along each side of body. **LENGTH:** 3–5½". **HABITAT:** Sandy deserts, washes, roadsides. **RANGE:** Western and southwestern U.S.

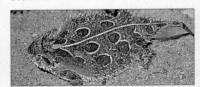

ROUND-TAILED HORNED LIZARD
Phrynosoma modestum

LOOK FOR: A tan to gray horned lizard with 4 short horns of equal length on its crown and a round tail; no pointed scales along sides. **LENGTH:** 3–4". **HABITAT:** Gravel, or rocky deserts, brushlands, and grasslands. **RANGE:** Southwestern U.S.

TEXAS HORNED LIZARD
Phrynosoma cornutum

LOOK FOR: A horned lizard with ringed spots on back, 2 long central spines in crown, 2 rows of pointed scales along sides, and keels on belly scales. **LENGTH:** 2½–7". **HABITAT:** Open, sandy to gravelly grasslands and deserts. **RANGE:** South-central to southwestern U.S.

FIVE-LINED SKINK
Eumeces fasciatus

The Five-lined Skink is a common visitor to rock gardens, patios, and woodsheds. It is quite agile and difficult to catch. The juvenile's bright blue tail is an anti-predator device. It breaks off easily and twitches for a period of time. This draws the predator's attention to the tail and often allows the skink to escape an attacking bird, snake, or larger lizard. The tail then grows back.

LOOK FOR: A shiny-scaled black lizard with 5 yellowish stripes and a blue tail. Older skinks lose stripes; blue tail fades to dull purple or brown. Males turn all brown with an orange head.

BROAD-HEADED SKINK
Eumeces laticeps

LOOK FOR: A tree-climbing skink very similar to the Five-lined but larger. Stripes and blue tail fade with age, and male develops orange head with swollen cheeks. **LENGTH:** 6½–12". **HABITAT:** Forests with logs, stumps, and tree holes. **RANGE:** Pennsylvania to Kansas, south to Texas and Florida.

COAL SKINK
Eumeces anthracinus

LOOK FOR: A 4-lined skink with broad, light-edged side stripes running from the eye onto the tail. **LENGTH:** 5–7". **HABITAT:** Moist, rocky woodlands near springs and streams. **RANGE:** Southwestern U.S.; scattered populations in East.

GROUND SKINK
Scincella lateralis

LOOK FOR: A small, short-legged, tan to reddish-brown skink with a dark stripe on each side from nose to tail. **LENGTH:** 3–5½". **HABITAT:** Woodlands, rocky hillsides, fields, gardens, trash heaps. **RANGE:** New Jersey to Nebraska, south to Texas and Florida.

ADULT

LENGTH: 5–8½".

HABITAT: Damp woodlands, hardwood forests, pine woods, gardens, sawdust heaps.

RANGE:

91

WESTERN SKINK
Eumeces skiltonianus

The Western Skink is difficult to see without exploring its hiding places under logs, stones, and debris. These skinks are most active in late afternoon and can be heard rustling about in search of beetles, crickets, spiders, and sow bugs. The tail breaks if grabbed.

LOOK FOR: A shiny-scaled lizard with a broad brown stripe down the back bordered by whitish or beige stripes that begin on the nose and end on the tail. Young have blue tail; fades to gray or brown.

LENGTH: 6½–9".

HABITAT: Rocky areas near streams,

grasslands, woodlands, forest
clearings, dry hillsides.

RANGE:

GREAT PLAINS SKINK
Eumeces obsoletus
LOOK FOR: A large skink with black-edged
brown scales. Scales on sides in diagonal
rows. Young are black with blue tail, white
spots around mouth. **LENGTH:** 6½–13". **HABITAT:**
Grasslands, woodlands; usually near rivers
in dry prairies and deserts. **RANGE:** Southern
Nebraska to Arizona and southern Texas.

GILBERT'S SKINK
Eumeces gilberti
LOOK FOR: Plain brown or olive skink with
dark spotting. Young have blue or red tail
and white stripes on sides. **LENGTH:** 7–12".
HABITAT: Rocky areas near springs and
streams, grasslands, deserts, pine forests.
RANGE: Central California to Arizona.

MANY-LINED SKINK
Eumeces multivirgatus
LOOK FOR: A thin skink with short legs, very
long tail, and light and dark lines
(sometimes stripeless). **LENGTH:** 5–7½". **HABITAT:**
From deserts and prairies to mountain
forests, canyon streamsides, and vacant
lots. **RANGE:** Central to southwestern U.S.

SIX-LINED RACERUNNER
Cnemidophorus sexlineatus

The Six-lined Racerunner and its kin, the whiptails, are known for their speed. These lizards like hot weather; they are the last ones to become active in spring and the first to retreat in the fall. Racerunners are active during the heat of the day when other lizards have disappeared. They depend on speed to catch insects and avoid predators.

LOOK FOR: A very fast, nervous, long-tailed lizard with 6 light stripes running length of brown or greenish-brown body.

LENGTH: 6–9½".

HABITAT: Dry, sunny fields, coastal

dunes, woodland edges,
grasslands, river floodplains.
RANGE:

WESTERN WHIPTAIL
Cnemidophorus tigris
LOOK FOR: A lizard with a network of bars,
spots, and faded stripes on back. Scattered
black spots on throat and chest. **LENGTH:**
8–12". **HABITAT:** Open deserts with shrubs.
RANGE: Eastern Oregon and southern Idaho
to Baja California and western Texas.

CHECKERED WHIPTAIL
Cnemidophorus tesselatus
LOOK FOR: A whiptail with checkered black
spots and bars on back; noticeably enlarged
scales in front of throat fold. **LENGTH:** 11–15".
HABITAT: Rocky deserts, gullies, canyon
slopes with little vegetation. **RANGE:**
Southwestern U.S.

TEXAS SPOTTED WHIPTAIL
Cnemidophorus gularis
LOOK FOR: A whiptail with 7 or 8 light stripes
and white spots between side stripes. Male
has pink or orange throat, blue-black
belly. **LENGTH:** 6½"–11". **HABITAT:** Rocky
hillsides, short-grass prairies, along river
courses. **RANGE:** Southwestern U.S.

SOUTHERN ALLIGATOR LIZARD
Elgaria multicarinata

Alligator lizards are covered with heavy scales reinforced with bony plates. A fold of skin along each side of the body allows these lizards to expand after eating a huge meal or when females are swollen with eggs. These lizards are usually found under logs and rocks, but occasionally they climb into brush, aided by their stiff tails. Look for them in sunny forest glades.

Look for: A slim-bodied, long-tailed lizard with yellow eyes, short legs, and a well-defined fold on each side of its body. Dark bands across back and tail; faint lengthwise dashes or stripes down middle rows of scales on belly.

Length: 10–16".

Habitat: Coastal oak woodlands and chaparral, grasslands, moist canyon bottoms.

Range:

NORTHERN ALLIGATOR LIZARD
Elgaria coerulea

LOOK FOR: A brown-eyed alligator lizard with faint irregular bands across back and tail and dark stripes on belly between rows of scales. **LENGTH:** 8–13". **HABITAT:** Woodlands and forest clearings. **RANGE:** Southern British Columbia and northwestern U.S.

ARIZONA ALLIGATOR LIZARD
Elgaria kingii

LOOK FOR: An alligator lizard with black and white spots on snout and bold banding across body and tail. No belly stripes. **LENGTH:** 7½–12". **HABITAT:** Woodlands, canyon bottoms, creosote bush deserts. **RANGE:** Central and southeastern Arizona and southwestern New Mexico.

GILA MONSTER
Heloderma suspectum

The Gila (pronounced HEE-la) Monster is one of only two venomous lizards. (The other is the Mexican Beaded Lizard.) Gila Monsters return to the same feeding and wintering areas year after year. In spring the males engage in spectacular wrestling matches to gain access to females. The Gila Monster spends more than 90 percent of its time underground. It eats the eggs of birds and reptiles, nesting birds, and small mammals.

LOOK FOR: A large, stocky, slow-moving lizard with broad head, black snout, and sausage-shaped tail. Body covered with small round scales that look like tiny beads. Black with pattern of pink, orange, or yellow.

LENGTH: 18–24".

HABITAT: Desert scrub, rocky foothills, oak woodlands, canyons.

RANGE:

CAUTION: Venomous bite causes severe pain and localized swelling. Not known to be fatal to humans.

CHUCKWALLA
Sauromalus obesus

LOOK FOR: A large, big-bellied lizard with a thick, tapering tail. Skin appears loose around neck and sides. Male has black head, shoulders, and legs. Female and young have dark and light bands across body. Harmless. **LENGTH:** 11–16". **HABITAT:** Lava flows, rock outcrops, rocky hillsides in creosote bush desert. **RANGE:** Southern California to southern Utah and western Arizona.

EASTERN GLASS LIZARD
Ophisaurus ventralis

These long, legless lizards are often mistaken for snakes. They move as snakes do, but look closely and you'll see eyelids and ear openings—not found in snakes. Glass lizards have scales stiffened by small, bony plates, which makes them feel brittle. Their long, fragile tails snap easily, and few adults have their original tails. Like alligator lizards, they have a fold along the side that allows them to expand. Females lay their eggs in moist cavities under logs and coil over them to protect them while they develop.

LOOK FOR: A large, legless lizard with a fold in the skin along each side. Adults black with square green spots; young tan with dark stripes. Belly yellow. Scales on back have pale dots on edges.

SLENDER GLASS LIZARD
Ophisaurus attenuatus

LOOK FOR: A brownish glass lizard with a dark back stripe and stripes below fold on sides and under tail. **LENGTH:** 22–42". **HABITAT:** Open woodlands and dry grasslands. **RANGE:** Southeastern and central U.S. from Wisconsin to eastern Texas.

CALIFORNIA LEGLESS LIZARD
Anniella pulchra

LOOK FOR: A shiny legless lizard with no ear openings. Silver above, yellow below. **LENGTH:** 6–9". **HABITAT:** Areas with sand or loose soil, beach dunes, chaparral, woodlands. **RANGE:** Western California.

FLORIDA WORM LIZARD
Rhineura floridana

LOOK FOR: A pink, wormlike lizard with no eyes, ears, or legs. Scales arranged in rings. **LENGTH:** 7–16". **HABITAT:** Dry oak woodlands and sandhills. **RANGE:** Northern and central Florida.

LENGTH: 18–43".

HABITAT: Flatwoods, wet meadows, sand dunes, coastal forests, moist hammocks, vacant lots.

RANGE:

WESTERN BLIND SNAKE
Leptotyphlops humilis

Blind snakes are often called worm snakes because of their resemblance to earthworms. Although they have black spots where the eyes would be, they are blind, able only to distinguish light and dark. They track ants and termites to their nests by following their scent trails.

Look for: A small, shiny, purplish or silvery snake. Tips of head and tail rounded; spine at tip of tail. One scale between black eye spots.

Length: 7–16".

Habitat: Deserts, grasslands, rocky

BRAHMINY BLIND SNAKE
Ramphotyphlops braminus

LOOK FOR: A tiny, slender, wormlike snake with a short, blunt tail. Gray, brown, or black back and lighter belly. **LENGTH:** 5–6½".
HABITAT: Shady gardens and areas with loose, moist soils. **RANGE:** Introduced to southern Florida and Hawaii.

hillsides along streams where soils permit burrowing.

RANGE:

The Rubber Boa is related to the giant snakes of South America, the Anaconda and Boa Constrictor. All these snakes have a small spur on each side where legs would be. Rubber Boas are constrictors and feed primarily on rodents and shrews. They are active at night and give birth to live young.

LOOK FOR: A rubbery-looking, plain olive, rich brown, or pink snake. Body stout; head and short tail

Rosy Boa
Lichanura trivirgata

Look for: A thick, smooth snake with blunt head and tail. Slate gray or rosy beige with 3 broad irregular-edged brown stripes. Small eyes, vertical pupils. **Length:** 24–42". **Habitat:** Deserts, rocky brushlands near streams and springs. **Range:** Southern California and southwestern Arizona into Mexico.

rounded off at tips. Eyes small, with vertical pupils.

Length: 14–33".

Habitat: Near water, grasslands, deserts, woodlands, mountain forests.

Range:

COMMON GARTER SNAKE
Thamnophis sirtalis

The Common Garter Snake is the most wide-ranging and commonly seen snake in the United States and Canada, where a dozen species of garter snakes are found. In northern areas, thousands of Common Garter Snakes may gather together to spend the winter in a communal den. During the day, this snake prowls for worms and amphibians. Garter snakes may bite when first handled, but they tame quickly.

LOOK FOR: A snake with 3 stripes down the back. Color and pattern can vary significantly. Stripes are often yellow with black between them. There may be red or black spots between the stripes. Some have no stripes at all.

Length: 18–51".

Habitat: Near water, parks, farms, gardens, meadows, marshes, woodlands.

Range:

EASTERN RIBBON SNAKE
Thamnophis sauritus

Look for: A slim, long-tailed garter snake with 3 bold stripes of yellow, tan, orange or pale blue (color depends on age and region). **Length:** 18–40". **Habitat:** Streamsides, wet meadows, marshes, ponds. **Range:** Southeastern Canada, eastern U.S.

WESTERN RIBBON SNAKE
Thamnophis proximus

Look for: Similar to eastern relative, with large pair of joined spots on top of head. **Length:** 19–47". **Habitat:** Streamsides, lake shallows, marshes, weedy ponds. **Range:** Central U.S.

LINED SNAKE
Tropidoclonion lineatum

Look for: A garter snake look-alike with 3 distinct stripes. Two rows of black half-moons down middle of belly. **Length:** 7½–21". **Habitat:** Woodland edges, prairie hillsides, vacant lots, trash heaps. **Range:** Scattered in central U.S.

WESTERN TERRESTRIAL GARTER SNAKE
Thamnophis elegans

Identifying Western Terrestrial Garter Snakes is a challenge, even for herpetologists, because this species displays extraordinary color and pattern variation across its range. These snakes forage in trees, on land, or in water for slugs, leeches, fish, frogs, lizards, snakes, birds, mice, and bats.

LOOK FOR: A garter snake with a distinct back stripe, less distinct side stripes. Checkered spotting or white flecks between stripes.

LENGTH: 18–43".

RED-SIDED GARTER SNAKE
Thamnophis sirtalis parietalis

LOOK FOR: Western race of Common Garter Snake with red or orange spots between stripes. **LENGTH:** 16–48". **HABITAT:** Meadows, ditches, ponds, streamsides. **RANGE:** Western North America, Great Plains.

PLAINS GARTER SNAKE
Thamnophis radix

LOOK FOR: A garter snake with a yellow to orange back stripe and 2 rows of black checks between side and back stripes. **LENGTH:** 20–40". **HABITAT:** Prairie marshes, pond edges, river valleys. **RANGE:** Great Plains.

CHECKERED GARTER SNAKE
Thamnophis marcianus

LOOK FOR: A garter snake with checkerboard pattern on sides. Pair of black blotches on sides of head separated from eye by pale half-moon shapes. **LENGTH:** 18–42". **HABITAT:** Marshes, streamsides, pond edges, springs. **RANGE:** South-central to southwestern U.S.

HABITAT: Grasslands, woodlands, usually near wetlands.

RANGE:

109

NORTHERN WATER SNAKE
Nerodia sipedon

The Northern Water Snake is one of the most common species of water snake. Fishermen often mistakenly blame this snake for eating all the game fish, but it eats mostly small fishes and frogs. In spring and early summer, these snakes are most often seen basking on branches overhanging water or on debris at the water's edge. During hot weather they come out only at night. Young, perhaps 10 to 50 in number, are born alive.

LOOK FOR: A thick-bodied, rough-skinned snake with a dark band around its neck, dark blotches on its back and sides, and half-moon spots on its belly.

LENGTH: 22–59".

SOUTHERN WATER SNAKE
Nerodia fasciata

LOOK FOR: A banded water snake with a dark line from eye to corner of mouth and squiggles or squares on belly. **LENGTH:** 24–62". **HABITAT:** Most freshwater wetlands. **RANGE:** Southeastern U.S.

BROWN WATER SNAKE
Nerodia taxispilota

LOOK FOR: A large water snake with a row of dark brown blotches on midback and each side. **LENGTH:** 30–69". **HABITAT:** Large swamps, rivers, lakes, where vegetation overhangs water. **RANGE:** Southeastern U.S.

DIAMOND-BACKED WATER SNAKE
Nerodia rhombifer

LOOK FOR: A water snake with a chainlike pattern and yellowish belly. **LENGTH:** 30–63". **HABITAT:** Swamps, marshes, lakes. **RANGE:** South-central and southwestern U.S.

HABITAT: Ponds, lakes, streams, rivers, marshes, ditches, swamps.

RANGE:

CAUTION: All water snakes tend to be nasty and quick to bite.

111

PLAIN-BELLIED WATER SNAKE
Nerodia erythrogaster

The Plain-bellied Water Snake is active by day and night in warm weather. Although mainly seen in streams, ponds, and other freshwater bodies, it is occasionally found under debris some distance from water. Like most water snakes, this species is feisty if handled.

LOOK FOR: A water snake with a brown, green, or gray back and a solid red, orange, or yellow belly. In West, may have light bands with dark borders across its back.

LENGTH: 30–62".

HABITAT: Swamps, slow streams, ponds, lakes.

MISSISSIPPI GREEN WATER SNAKE
Nerodia cyclopion

LOOK FOR: A greenish water snake with a muted pattern of spotting on back. Light half-moon marks on belly. Similar Florida Green Snake of Southeast has plain belly. **LENGTH:** 30–50". **HABITAT:** Quiet or very slow waters. **RANGE:** Lower Mississippi Valley.

QUEEN SNAKE
Regina septemvittata

LOOK FOR: A brown water snake with a yellow stripe on each side and 4 brown stripes on yellow belly. **LENGTH:** 15–36". **HABITAT:** Shallow rocky streams with crayfish. **RANGE:** Ontario and Michigan to Florida panhandle.

GRAHAM'S CRAYFISH SNAKE
Regina grahamii

LOOK FOR: A brown water snake with a wide yellow side stripe. Yellowish belly may have a central row of dark spots. **LENGTH:** 18–47". **HABITAT:** Ponds, slow prairie streams, marshes. **RANGE:** Midwest to southern U.S.

RANGE:

CAUTION: This species will bite a captor repeatedly and secrete a foul-smelling musk.

113

RED-BELLIED SNAKE
Storeria occipitomaculata

Shy, secretive, and active mainly at night, the Red-bellied Snake is not often seen. During the day it hides under rocks, boards, and woodland litter. Slugs are its favorite food. It hibernates with brown, garter, and green snakes in deserted ant mounds and rodent burrows. It is not known to bite.

Look for: A small reddish-brown or gray snake with 1 wide light stripe or 4 thin stripes running length of back, or both. Belly usually red to yellow, sometimes black.

Length: 8–16".

Habitat: Open forests, old fields, wood lots, wetland edges.

Range:

BROWN SNAKE
Storeria dekayi

Look for: A snake with a row of brown spots on each side of tan back stripe. Dark spot under eye and side of neck. **Length:** 9–20".
Habitat: Lots, gardens, grasslands, forests.
Range: Southern Canada to eastern U.S.

KIRTLAND'S SNAKE
Clonophis kirtlandii

Look for: A snake with 2 rows of large dark spots on sides. Brick red belly scales edged with row of black spots. **Length:** 14–24".
Habitat: Wet meadows, swamps. **Range:** Great Lakes and midwestern U.S.

BLACK SWAMP SNAKE
Seminatrix pygaea

Look for: A shiny black water snake with a red belly and tiny pale streaks on smooth back scales. **Length:** 10–18". **Habitat:** Swamps. ponds, mainly with water hyacinth. **Range:** Coastal southeastern U.S.

RINGNECK SNAKE
Diadophis punctatus

Like most small snakes, the Ringneck is shy and meek. It hides under flat stones and forest litter and looks for salamanders, small lizards, and earthworms to eat. Some western subspecies, including the Prairie Ringneck, will bury the head in the coils when alarmed and elevate the bright tail in corkscrew fashion. This may distract predators—and a bite to the tail has less chance of killing the snake than one to the head.

Look for: A black, gray, greenish, or brown snake with a yellow or orange neck ring (occasionally absent) and a bright red, yellow, or orange belly, sometimes with black spots.

Length: 10–30".

Habitat: Moist hardwood and mixed forests, grasslands, chaparral, desert streamsides.

Range:

EASTERN WORM SNAKE
Carphophis amoenus

Look for: A wormlike snake with a brown back and a pink belly. Spinelike scale at end of tail. **Length:** 7½–13". **Habitat:** Moist, rocky, wooded hillsides; forest edges. **Range:** Southern New England and central Georgia to southeastern Nebraska and northeastern Texas.

PINE WOODS SNAKE
Rhadinaea flavilata

Look for: A small yellowish-brown to reddish snake with a pale yellow to whitish belly. Dark line through eye. **Length:** 10–15". **Habitat:** Pine flatwoods, hammocks, coastal islands. **Range:** Coastal areas of North Carolina to eastern Louisiana and Florida.

Mud Snakes are rarely seen, except on rainy nights when they're crossing roads. They hide by day, and at night they burrow in mud and vegetation in search of eels and eel-like salamanders called amphiumas and sirens.

RAINBOW SNAKE
Farancia erytrogramma

Look for: A shiny, black, cylinder-shaped snake with 3 red stripes along back. Red belly with 2 rows of black spots. **Length:** 27–66". **Habitat:** Coastal creeks, rivers, marshes, ditches. **Range:** Coastal plain, Maryland to eastern Louisiana.

Look for: A shiny, smooth-scaled, blue-black snake with pink or red blotches on belly and sides. Body cylinder-shaped. Sharp tail tip.

Length: 40–81".

Habitat: Swamps, marshes, weedy slow streams and ponds.

Range:

119

ROUGH GREEN SNAKE
Opheodrys aestivus

LOOK FOR: A slender snake with a solid green back and plain yellow or pale green belly. Scales are keeled, making skin rough.

LENGTH: 20–45".

HABITAT: Lake edges, forests, old fields, thickets.

RANGE:

The Rough Green Snake is a tree-climber. It favors vegetation along lakes and streams. Herpetologists locate these snakes at night using a headlamp. Although Rough Green Snakes are difficult to spot by day, at night their skin reflects the beam of light, and their bodies, coiled around branches, are easy to spot. These snakes eat insects and spiders.

SMOOTH GREEN SNAKE
Liochlorophis vernalis

LOOK FOR: A small snake with a uniformly green back and a yellowish-green to white belly. Scales smooth, without keels. Seen during the day. **LENGTH:** 14–26". **HABITAT:** Grassy fields, meadows, marshes. **RANGE:** Southeastern Canada to northeastern and north-central U.S.; scattered in West.

GREEN RAT SNAKE
Senticolis triaspis

LOOK FOR: A slim green to gray-green snake with a whitish belly. Long head with square snout. Often climbs shrubs and small trees. **LENGTH:** 24–50". **HABITAT:** Near streams in wooded rocky canyons. **RANGE:** Southeastern Arizona into Mexico.

121

SOUTHEASTERN CROWNED SNAKE
Tantilla coronata

The Southeastern Crowned Snake, like other members of its genus, is a nocturnal, secretive burrower and is usually found under stones and inside rotted logs and stumps. These snakes don't bite when captured. They do, however, have small venom glands and enlarged rear teeth, and their bite is believed to disable their prey—centipedes, spiders, and termites.

FLAT-HEADED SNAKE
Tantilla gracilis

LOOK FOR: A small, shiny snake. Reddish-brown, tan, or gray back. Pinkish or orange belly. Head darker than body. **LENGTH:** 7–9½". **HABITAT:** Woodlands, grasslands. **RANGE:** Central and south-central U.S.

PLAINS BLACK-HEADED SNAKE
Tantilla nigriceps

LOOK FOR: A solid brown snake with a black patch on top of head that is pointed toward rear. **LENGTH:** 7–15". **HABITAT:** Dry woodlands, grasslands, rocky brushlands. **RANGE:** Southwestern U.S.

SOUTHWESTERN BLACK-HEADED SNAKE
Tantilla hobartsmithi

LOOK FOR: A brown snake with a black patch on head that is straight at rear. **LENGTH:** 7–12". **HABITAT:** Dry, open, rocky brushlands to dry open forests. **RANGE:** Scattered populations in southwestern U.S.

LOOK FOR: A snake with a dark brown to black head crown, a light neck band, and an unpatterned tan to dark brown body. Cream to pinkish belly.

LENGTH: 8–13".

HABITAT: Dry pine forests, sandhills, open woodlands, forest edges.

RANGE:

EASTERN HOGNOSE SNAKE
Heterodon platirhinos

Hognose snakes go through a whole catalog of tricks to get rid of a foe. If you come close to one it will try to scare you off by hissing, puffing itself up, flattening its head, and spreading its neck. If that doesn't work, it rolls over on its back, sticks out its tongue, convulses, and then lies still as if dead. The Eastern Hognose Snake eats toads.

Look for: A snake with an upturned nose and a thick neck. Pattern and color vary; normally spotted, but occasionally jet black. Tail light-colored below; belly darker.

Length: 20–45".

Habitat: Sandy areas, fields,

SOUTHERN HOGNOSE SNAKE
Heterodon simus

LOOK FOR: A short, stout snake with a sharply upturned snout. Belly and underside of tail light gray or yellowish. **LENGTH:** 14–24". **HABITAT:** Sandhills, pine flatwoods, dry woodlands. **RANGE:** Southeastern U.S.

grasslands, woodland edges, pine woods, barrier beaches.

RANGE:

WESTERN HOGNOSE SNAKE
Heterodon nasicus

LOOK FOR: A snake with a turned-up snout. Belly and underside of tail mostly black. **LENGTH:** 15–39". **HABITAT:** Sandy dry prairies. **RANGE:** Southeastern Alberta and southwestern Manitoba to southeastern Arizona and Texas, scattered populations eastward.

WESTERN PATCH-NOSED SNAKE
Salvadora hexalepis

Western Patch-nosed Snakes are very active in the daytime, like racers and whipsnakes. They are mostly ground-dwellers and move rapidly. To regulate their temperature, they may bask in the open or bury themselves in warm sand. Lizards and reptile eggs are favorite foods, and the "patch nose" may be an adaptation for excavating eggs. They do most of their foraging in the morning and late afternoon, when lizards are active.

LOOK FOR: A slim gray snake with a wide, triangle-shaped scale on its nose, curving back over the snout. Tan to yellow stripe down center of back with dark stripe on either side.

WESTERN HOOK-NOSED SNAKE
Gyalopion canum

LOOK FOR: A tan snake with brown rings and a turned-up snout. **LENGTH:** 7–14". **HABITAT:** Deserts, grassy foothills, pinyon-juniper woodlands. **RANGE:** Western Texas to southeastern Arizona and southward.

SPOTTED LEAF-NOSED SNAKE
Phyllorhynchus decurtatus

LOOK FOR: A snake with a triangular patch on snout and brown blotches down center of back. Vertical pupils. **LENGTH:** 12–20". **HABITAT:** Dry, open plains, creosote bush deserts. **RANGE:** Southern Nevada, southern California, southwestern Arizona, and southward.

LENGTH: 20–46".

HABITAT: Desert brushlands, dry grasslands, chaparral, dry woodlands.

RANGE:

NIGHT SNAKE
Hypsiglena torquata

The Night Snake is at home in a wide variety of climates, from the temperate northwestern United States to tropical Mexico. Like other snakes that are active after dark, it has vertical pupils. It is seen most frequently crossing warm back roads at night. It feeds on lizards, snakes, and frogs. While harmless to humans, the Night Snake has enlarged, grooved teeth that hold prey while a mild venom subdues it.

LOOK FOR: A tan to gray snake with dark spots on back and a pair of large dark blotches on the neck. Vertical pupils.

LENGTH: 12–26".

LYRE SNAKE

Trimorphodon biscutatus

LOOK FOR: A tan or gray snake with blotches on back and a broad head with a lyre- or wishbone-shaped mark. Pupils vertical.
LENGTH: 18–47". **HABITAT:** Deserts, grasslands, rocky hills, canyons, mountain forests.
RANGE: Southern California, Nevada, and Utah to western Texas.

CAT-EYED SNAKE

Leptodeira septentrionalis

LOOK FOR: A tan to reddish snake with dark brown or black blotches crossing back. Vertical pupils. Head much wider than neck. **LENGTH:** 18–38". **HABITAT:** Near water, coastal plains and dry lands in Texas.
RANGE: Southern Texas to South America.

HABITAT: Deserts, grasslands, chaparral, brushlands, mountain meadows.

RANGE:

BLACK RAT SNAKE
Elaphe obsoleta obsoleta

Rat snakes are large, powerful constrictors and excellent climbers. They are often found in barns and falling-down old buildings, where their shed skins may be draped in the rafters. As the name suggests, rat snakes eat rodents, as well as rabbits, birds, and eggs. Out and about during the day in spring and fall, they often don't move until just after sunset in summer. They sometimes hole up for the winter with Copperheads or Timber Rattlesnakes.

LOOK FOR: A large, stout snake with a flat belly and straight sides, giving it a squarish shape. Occurs in 3 main color patterns. Northern adults: plain black (pictured here). Coastal southeast adults: yellow, greenish, or orange, with 4 stripes. Southern adults: yellowish or gray with blotches.

LENGTH: 42–101".

HABITAT: Farm fields, hardwood forests, rocky hillsides, swamps, marsh edges.

RANGE:

YELLOW RAT SNAKE
Elaphe obsoleta quadrivittata

LOOK FOR: A yellow snake with 4 dark stripes. **LENGTH:** 42–87". **HABITAT:** Coastal marshes and forests, flatwoods, old farms. **RANGE:** Southeastern coast of U.S.

GRAY RAT SNAKE
Elaphe obsoleta spiloides

LOOK FOR: A snake with gray or brown blotches on lighter background. **LENGTH:** 42–84". **HABITAT:** Hardwood forests, farms, wetland edges. **RANGE:** Mississippi Valley to southeastern U.S.

TEXAS RAT SNAKE
Elaphe obsoleta lindheimerii

LOOK FOR: A snake with brown or black blotches on yellow or grayish background. **LENGTH:** 42–86". **HABITAT:** Swamps, briar patches, farms. **RANGE:** Louisiana to central and southern Texas.

131

CORN SNAKE
Elaphe guttata

Corn Snakes are good at rodent-control around barns and old houses with broken stone foundations, where mice are abundant. Unfortunately, people often mistake these snakes for Copperheads and kill them on sight. In summer Corn Snakes are active at night. They spend their days in old stumps, rock walls, or abandoned burrows. When cornered, the Corn Snake will vibrate its tail and strike with impressive speed.

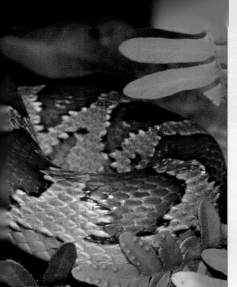

LOOK FOR: An orange to light gray snake with big, black-edged, red, brown, or dark gray blotches on its back. Blotch on head comes to a point between eyes. Tail striped below, belly marked with black squares. Scales are keeled.

LENGTH: 30–72".

HABITAT: Pine barrens, open woodlands, old fields, farm buildings, trash heaps.

RANGE:

FOX SNAKE
Elaphe vulpina

LOOK FOR: A snake with an orange head and dark blotches on back. Dark squares on belly. Keeled scales. **LENGTH:** 36–70". **HABITAT:** Farms, woods, prairies, marshes. **RANGE:** Great Lakes to north-central U.S.

PRAIRIE KINGSNAKE
Lampropeltis calligaster calligaster

LOOK FOR: A snake with shiny, smooth scales and many close-set blotches down back. Pattern fades with age. **LENGTH:** 30–56". **HABITAT:** Old fields, pine woods, farms. **RANGE:** Central to south-central U.S.

MOLE KINGSNAKE
Lampropeltis calligaster rhombomaculata

LOOK FOR: A snake with shiny, smooth scales and reddish-brown, black-edged spots down back. **LENGTH:** 30–56". **HABITAT:** Fields, woodlands, farms. **RANGE:** Southeastern U.S., except Florida peninsula.

133

NORTHERN BLACK RACER
Coluber constrictor constrictor

Gone in a flash! Racers are long, slender, agile, fast-moving snakes. They are frequently found basking in trees and shrubs. Once warmed, they cruise for grasshoppers, frogs, lizards, and mice, with their heads held high to get a better view of their surroundings. When prey is spotted, they make a quick dash for it. Racers are not constrictors and repeatedly bite the prey until it is subdued. Racers return to the same dens each fall, and often share them with other snake species.

LOOK FOR: A shiny, all black to bluish snake with white or gray chin and throat and gray to yellow belly. Smooth scales. Large eyes.

BLUE RACER
Coluber constrictor foxi

LOOK FOR: A pale bluish-gray or bluish-green snake with a bluish or white belly. **LENGTH:** 36–72". **HABITAT:** Bogs, lake edges, open woods, prairies. **RANGE:** Great Lakes region.

YELLOW-BELLIED RACER
Coluber constrictor flaviventris

LOOK FOR: A light blue, blue-green, gray, or brown snake with a yellowish belly. **LENGTH:** 23–70". **HABITAT:** Grasslands, open woods. **RANGE:** Central U.S.

EASTERN INDIGO SNAKE
Drymarchon corais couperi

LOOK FOR: A very long, shiny snake that is bluish-black top and bottom. Chin and sides of head often reddish. Smooth scales. **LENGTH:** 60–103". **HABITAT:** Gopher tortoise burrows; pine woods and palmetto thickets near water. **RANGE:** Southeastern U.S.

LENGTH: 36–73".

HABITAT: Open hardwood forests, old fields, grasslands, prairies, marsh edges.

RANGE:

EASTERN COACHWHIP
Masticophis flagellum flagellum

The Eastern Coachwhip rivals the racer for North America's fastest snake. If approached it disappears in a burst of speed into a burrow or rocky crevice. It prowls for and subdues prey as racers do. If taken by surprise and cornered, it defensively coils, shakes its tail, and may advance toward the aggressor. If grabbed, it will bite hard, hold on, and chew.

LOOK FOR: A large, lean, long-tailed speedster. Dark brown head and neck fading to light brown body (east); or tan, yellow, brown, or reddish with dark crossbars on neck (west).

LENGTH: 42–102".

HABITAT: Pine flatwoods, open wooded hillsides, grasslands, deserts, chaparral.

RANGE:

RED COACHWHIP
Masticophis flagellum piceus

LOOK FOR: A reddish or salmon-pink whiplike snake with band around neck. **LENGTH:** 42–102". **HABITAT:** Dry brushlands, prairie, dry open woodlands. **RANGE:** Southwestern U.S.

STRIPED WHIPSNAKE
Masticophis taeniatus

LOOK FOR: A gray snake with a white side stripe broken by fine black lines or dashes. **LENGTH:** 36–72". **HABITAT:** Rocky streamsides, canyons, flatlands to mountains. **RANGE:** Western and southwestern U.S.

STRIPED RACER
Masticophis lateralis

LOOK FOR: A dark whiplike snake with a cream, yellow, or orange side stripe. Tail pink below. **LENGTH:** 30–60". **HABITAT:** Chaparral, rocky hillsides, gullies. **RANGE:** California.

137

BULLSNAKE/GOPHER SNAKE
Pituophis catenifer sayi

The Bullsnake, a subspecies of the Gopher Snake, is quite the actor, putting on an impressive impersonation of a rattlesnake when threatened. It flattens its head, puffs up its body, shakes its tail, hisses loudly, and strikes repeatedly. There are many subspecies of Gopher Snakes, and they vary considerably in color and pattern. They eat lots of rats and mice. In winter, they may share their dens with rattlesnakes, racers, whipsnakes, and garter snakes.

LOOK FOR: A large, robust snake with a relatively small head and a somewhat pointed snout. Dark bar from eye to corner of the mouth. Scales are keeled.

LENGTH: 36–100".

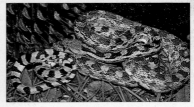

PACIFIC GOPHER SNAKE
Pituophis catenifer catenifer

LOOK FOR: A Gopher Snake with gray dots on side of body and underside of tail. **LENGTH:** 48–100". **HABITAT:** Grasslands to dry, open forests. **RANGE:** West Coast from Washington to central California.

FLORIDA PINE SNAKE
Pituophis melanoleucus mugitis

LOOK FOR: A large grayish snake with a small head and keeled scales. **LENGTH:** 48–83". **HABITAT:** Pine woods. **RANGE:** Southeastern U.S. from South Carolina to Florida.

GLOSSY SNAKE
Arizona elegans

LOOK FOR: A faded-looking snake with glossy scales. Protruding top jaw. **LENGTH:** 26–70". **HABITAT:** Deserts, grasslands, dry woodlands. **RANGE:** Southwestern U.S.

HABITAT: Pine barrens, sandhills (east), grasslands (midwest), brushlands, farms, open woodlands (west).

RANGE:

139

LONG-NOSED SNAKE
Rhinocheilus lecontei

Long-nosed Snakes are excellent burrowers in loose, sandy soils, yet they prefer to hide under surface debris or in rodent burrows during the day. They appear to be most active in the early evening. These snakes kill lizards, other snakes, and small mammals by constriction.

LOOK FOR: A tricolor snake with black saddles outlined with white spots on the sides, often alternating with red bands. White to yellow belly with a few dark spots. Long, pointed snout.

WESTERN SHOVEL-NOSED SNAKE
Chionactis occipitalis

LOOK FOR: A snake with black and red saddle-shaped marks and a shovel-shaped snout.
LENGTH: 10–17". **HABITAT:** Sandy deserts, rocky hillsides. **RANGE:** Southwestern U.S.

BANDED SAND SNAKE
Chilomeniscus cinctus

LOOK FOR: A tiny black and orange snake with a flat, spadelike snout. Small upturned eyes. **LENGTH:** 7–10". **HABITAT:** Deserts. **RANGE:** Southwestern Arizona into Mexico.

GROUND SNAKE
Sonora semiannulata

LOOK FOR: A small snake with black bands and red back stripe (sometimes plain). Small dark mark on front of each scale. **LENGTH:** 8–18". **HABITAT:** River bottoms, desert flats, rocky hillsides. **RANGE:** Western and south-central U.S.

LENGTH: 22–41".

HABITAT: Prairies, brushlands, deserts.

RANGE:

141

EASTERN KINGSNAKE
Lampropeltis getula getula

Kingsnakes and Milk Snakes are powerful constrictors. They are most frequently found under boards, sheets of tin, and tar paper, and around abandoned buildings and old sawdust piles. In addition to rodents, they eat a great variety of snakes (including

DESERT KINGSNAKE
Lampropeltis getula splendida

LOOK FOR: A snake with a chainlike pattern surrounding dark blotches down back and speckled sides. **LENGTH:** 36-60". **HABITAT:** Along water courses. **RANGE:** Southwestern U.S.

venomous species), lizards, and amphibians. They seem to be immune to pit viper venom.

LOOK FOR: A large, shiny black or brown and white snake with chain links, bands, stripes, blotches, or speckles.

LENGTH: 36–82".

HABITAT: Dry woodlands, pine barrens, rocky wooded hillsides to swamp edges, coastal marshes to prairies, deserts, and chaparral.

RANGE:

EASTERN MILK SNAKE
Lampropeltis triangulum triangulum

LOOK FOR: A snake with a pale V on head and black-edged blotches on back. **LENGTH:** 24–52". **HABITAT:** Coastal wetlands, woodlands, rocky hillsides, fields. meadows, old fields. **RANGE:** Eastern U.S.

RED MILK SNAKE
Lampropeltis triangulum syspila

LOOK FOR: A snake with red blotches against yellowish background. **LENGTH:** 21–42". **HABITAT:** Rocky wooded hillsides, forest edges, farms. **RANGE:** Midwestern U.S.

143

EASTERN CORAL SNAKE
Micrurus fulvius

The Eastern Coral Snake is related to the cobras and can deliver a very serious bite. Its venom attacks the nerves and quickly incapacitates the lizards and snakes upon which this snake feeds. Coral snakes are secretive and difficult to find. Mostly, they're discovered by people raking leaves or moving wood piles. The Scarlet Snake and the Scarlet Kingsnake, shown at right, are harmless species that look like coral snakes, but have red snouts and black rings between

WESTERN CORAL SNAKE
Micruroides euryxanthus

LOOK FOR: A coral snake with a blunt black snout followed by a white or yellow band. Rings circle body. **LENGTH:** 13–21". **HABITAT:** River valleys with mesquite, deserts. **RANGE:** Southwestern U.S. **CAUTION:** Venomous!

SCARLET KINGSNAKE
Lampropeltis triangulum elapsoides

LOOK FOR: A banded snake with a pointed red snout. Red and yellow rings separated by black rings. Rings may be incomplete. **LENGTH:** 14–27". **HABITAT:** Flatwoods. **RANGE:** Southeastern U.S.

SCARLET SNAKE
Cemophora coccinea

LOOK FOR: A banded snake with a pointed red snout. Red and yellow bands separated by black bands. White belly. **LENGTH:** 14–32". **HABITAT:** Pine woods. **RANGE:** Southeastern U.S.

red and yellow rings. Remember: "Red touch yellow kill a fellow, red and black, friend of Jack."

LOOK FOR: A banded snake with a blunt black snout followed by a wide yellow band across head. Red and yellow rings touch each other. Rings completely circle body. Scales glossy.

LENGTH: 20–47".

HABITAT: Pine woods, lake edges, sandy open woods.

RANGE:

CAUTION: These snakes deliver a painful, venomous bite. Stay clear!

145

Copperheads, like rattlesnakes and the Cottonmouth, belong to the pit viper family. With their hollow fangs, deep facial heat-sensing pits between the nostrils and the eyes, and vertical pupils, they are superbly designed for sit-and-wait, low-light hunting. A pit viper will wait along a rodent or shrew trail—sometimes for days—until supper comes along. At night, its heat sensors detect the prey and guide the strike.

LOOK FOR: A snake with an unmarked coppery, orange, or rusty-red head. Series of brown to reddish- brown dumbbell- or hourglass-shaped saddles on body.

LENGTH: 24–53".

HABITAT: Rocky wooded hillsides, swamp edges, pine woods, near canyon springs.

RANGE:

CAUTION: Copperheads can deliver a painful, venomous bite. Steer clear of them!

COTTONMOUTH
Agkistrodon piscivorus

LOOK FOR: A very thick, dark-colored water snake. Patternless or with rough-edged bands. Flattened head. **LENGTH:** 30–75". **HABITAT:** Coastal marshes, cypress swamps, ponds, rivers. **RANGE:** Southeastern U.S.

MASSASAUGA
Sistrurus catenatus

LOOK FOR: A gray rattlesnake with a row of large dark blotches down back and smaller blotches on sides. **LENGTH:** 18–40". **HABITAT:** Swamps, marshes, wet meadows, bogs, grasslands. **RANGE:** Southern Canada and northeastern U.S. to Arizona.

PIGMY RATTLESNAKE
Sistrurus miliarius

LOOK FOR: A brown to light gray, small rattler with a thin tail and delicate rattle. **LENGTH:** 15–32". **HABITAT:** Near water, mixed forests, pine flatwoods. **RANGE:** Southeastern U.S.

TIMBER RATTLESNAKE
Crotalus horridus

Timber Rattlesnakes are heavy-bodied pit vipers with a prominent rattle at the end of the tail. They are remarkably shy and aren't quick to sound their alarm or strike, as the Prairie Rattler is. The Timber spends about 200 days (from early October to late April) in its den. During the active season, it spends much of its time motionless and waiting for a rodent to pass, or basking in the sun, which aids digestion. Females give birth in the fall and stay with their young for up to two weeks. The young follow scent trails of adults to the hibernating chamber.

LOOK FOR: A rattler with dark bands and a black tail. All-black individuals common in the Northeast. Southern snakes have a reddish or rusty back stripe.

LENGTH: 36–74".

PRAIRIE RATTLESNAKE
Crotalus viridis viridis

LOOK FOR: A rattler with oval blotches on back turning into rings near tail. Varies in color and pattern. **LENGTH:** 20–65". **HABITAT:** Grasslands, deserts, hillsides, pine forests, dunes. **RANGE:** Western Canada and U.S.

EASTERN DIAMONDBACK
Crotalus adamanteus

LOOK FOR: A large rattler with diamond-shaped blotches outlined by yellow scales. Two diagonal yellow stripes on face. **LENGTH:** 33–96". **HABITAT:** Sandhills, pine flatwoods, palmetto thickets, Gopher Tortoise burrows. **RANGE:** Southeastern U.S.

WESTERN DIAMONDBACK
Crotalus atrox

LOOK FOR: A large rattler with dark diamonds edged with white. Black and white banded tail. **LENGTH:** 30–84". **HABITAT:** Dry brushlands, rocky outcrops, desert foothills. **RANGE:** South-central and southwestern U.S.

How to use the reference section

The **Glossary**, which begins below, contains terms used by naturalists. If you run across a word in this book that you do not understand, check the glossary for a definition. Also in this section is a listing of **Resources**, including books, Web sites, and organizations devoted to North American reptiles, as well as a table for learning how to convert measurements to metrics. Finally, there is an **Index** of all the species covered in the field guide section of this book.

GLOSSARY

Amphibian
A class of cold-blooded vertebrates, including salamanders and frogs, that live much of their lives in water.

Bask
To warm the body by lying in the sun.

Brackish
Describes a mixture of salt and fresh water.

Brushlands
Dry habitats with small shrubs and other low-growing plants.

Burrow
A hole or tunnel dug in the ground for shelter.

Camouflage
Colors or patterns that help animals blend in with their environments.

Chaparral
A dry habitat of dense evergreen shrubs and small trees most common on hillsides of California.

Clutch
A nest of eggs.

Den
A safe hidden place, often an animal's home.

Endangered
In danger of becoming extinct.

Estuary
A passage where a river connects with the sea.

Evolve
To change from generation to generation. Living things evolve through time; this is how new species develop.

Extinct
Describes a plant or animal species that has died out completely.

Fertilize
To unite a male animal's sperm with a female's egg. The fertilized egg then develops into a new animal.

Flatwoods
Longleaf Pine forest that grows in flatlands (low elevations) of the Southeast.

Forage
To search for food.

Genus
A group of closely related species.

Granular
Describes scales that are grainlike or beadlike.

Grassland
An area of prairie or meadow grass, usually found on flat or rolling plains that are dry most of the year.

Habitat
The environment in which an animal lives.

Hammock
A raised area in a wetland that is high enough for trees to grow with their roots above water.

Herpetologist
A scientist who studies reptiles and amphibians.

Hibernation
A long deep sleep, usually over the winter, when an animal's heartbeat and breathing slow down and its body temperature drops.

Iris
The colored part of the eye that surrounds the pupil.

Juvenile
A young animal in the stage of growth between baby and adult.

Keel
A small, raised ridge, often on a scale or scute.

Larva
A young animal that has hatched from its egg but must go through other growth stages before it resembles an adult.

Marsh
Treeless wetlands that develop around slow-moving bodies of water.

Mollusk
An invertebrate (animal with no backbone) with a soft body and a hard shell, such as a clam or snail.

Musk
A substance with a strong, often foul, smell that animals produce.

Nocturnal
Active at night.

Predator
An animal that hunts and kills other animals for food.

Prey
An animal caught by predators for food.

Pupil
The opening in the eye that controls the intake of light by opening and closing.

Range
The geographic area where a species normally lives.

Sandhill
A woodland of pine and oak that grows on dry, sandy hills in the Southeast.

Scrub
A habitat of small trees and shrubs that form low thickets.

Scutes
The dry, horny plates that form a turtle's shell.

Species
Animals that look alike and can mate and produce young.

Temperate
A climate or habitat that is neither very cold nor very hot.

Territory
An area that an animal occupies and uses for nesting and feeding.

Threatened
Likely to become endangered.

Vegetation
Plant life.

Venomous
Able to pass venom into a victim through a bite.

Vertebrate
An animal with a backbone.

Wetlands
Land with a lot of water in the soil, such as a marsh, swamp, or bog.

RESOURCES

FOR FURTHER READING

Alligators and Crocodiles
John L. Behler and Deborah A. Behler
Voyageur Press, 1998

Amphibians and Reptiles of the Great Lakes Region
James H. Harding
University of Michigan Press, 1997

The Encyclopedia of Reptiles and Amphibians
Tim R. Halliday and Kraig Adler (Eds.)
Facts on File, Inc., 1986

National Audubon Society Field Guide to North American Reptiles and Amphibians
John L. Behler and F. Wayne King
Alfred A. Knopf, 1979

National Audubon Society Pocket Guide to Familiar Reptiles and Amphibians of North America
John L. Behler
Alfred A. Knopf, 1988

Peterson Field Guides: Reptiles and Amphibians of Eastern and Central North America
Roger Conant and Joseph T. Collins
Houghton Mifflin, 1991

Rattlesnakes
Lawrence M. Klauber
University of California Press, 1982

Snakes: The Evolution of Mystery in Nature
Harry W. Greene
University of California Press, 1997

Snakes in Question: The Smithsonian Answer Book
Carl H. Ernst and George R. Zug
Smithsonian Institution Press, 1996

Turtles of the United States
Carl H. Ernst, Jeffrey E. Lovich, and Roger W. Barbour
Smithsonian Institution Press, 1994

VIDEO

Bill Nye the Science Guy: Reptiles
Bill Nye
Walt Disney Home Video, 1995

ORGANIZATIONS

Arizona Herpetological Society
P.O. Box 66712
Phoenix, AZ 85082-1625
Tel: 602-894-1625
http://www.syspac.com/
~varney/NETSCAPE/AHA/
aha.html

Gainesville Herpetological Society
P.O. Box 140353
Gainesville, FL 62614-0353
E-mail: herps@afn.org
http://www.angelfire.com/fl/
GVlHerpSoc

Ringneck Snake   page 116

Eyes on Nature: Snakes
Jane P. Resnick
Kidsbooks, 1996

Eyewitness Books: Reptile
Colin McCarthy
Alfred A. Knopf, 1991

The Fascinating World of Snakes
Barron's Educational Series, Inc., 1993

Peterson Field Guides: Western Reptiles and Amphibians
Robert C. Stebbins
Houghton Mifflin, 1985

Ranger Rick Science Spectacular Series: The World of Reptiles
Darlyne Murawski
Newbridge Communications, Inc., 1996

National Audubon Society
700 Broadway
New York, NY 10003-9562
Tel: 800-274-4201
http://www.audubon.org

The Nature Conservancy
International Headquarters
1815 North Lynn Street
Arlington, VA 22209
Tel. 703-841-5300

Wildlife Conservation Society
Reptile Department
Bronx Zoo
Bronx, New York 10460
Tel. 718-220-5152
http://www.wcs.org

WEB SITES

Alligators, Crocodiles, Turtles, Venomous Snakes Web site:

http://www.flmnh.ufl.edu/
natsci/herpetology/
herpetology.htm

Audubon's "Educate Yourself" Web site:
http://www.audubon.org/
educate

Biosis Internet Resource Guide for Zoology—General Zoology:
http://www.york.biosis.org/
zrdocs/zoolinfo/grp_rept.
htm

Herp Link:
http://home.ptd.net/
~herplink/index.html

National Geographic's King Cobra Web site:
http://www.nationalgeo
graphic.com/features/97/
kingcobra

Snakes of North America Web site:
http://www.pitt.edu/~mcs2/
herp/SoNA.html

Society for the Study of Amphibians and Reptiles:
http://falcon.cc.ukans.edu/
~gpisani/SSAR.html

Turtle Trax:
http://www.turtles.org

University of Michigan Museum of Zoology's Animal Diversity Web:
http://www.oit.itd.umich.edu/
bio108

The World Wide Web Virtual Library—Herpetology:
http://cmgm.stanford.edu/
~meisen/herp

Make it metric

Here is a chart you can use to change measurements of size, distance, weight, and temperature to their metric equivalents.

	multiply by
inches to millimeters	25
inches to centimeters	2.5
feet to meters	0.3
yards to meters	0.9
miles to kilometers	1.6
square miles to square kilometers	2.6
ounces to grams	28.3
pounds to kilograms	.45
Fahrenheit to Centigrade	subtract 32 and multiply by .55

INDEX

Page numbers in **bold type** point to a reptile's page in the field guide.

Five-lined Skink (page 90) with head in sand

Red-eared Slider   page 66

INDEX

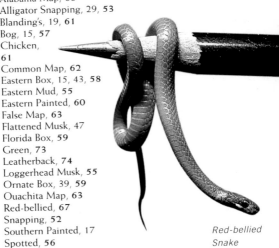

*Red-bellied
Snake
page 114*

PHOTO CREDITS

Credits are listed by page, from left to right, top to bottom.

69a: Karl H. Switak
69b: Lee Kline
70: James H. Harding
71a: Suzanne L. & Joseph T. Collins/Photo Researchers
71b: James H. Robinson
72: Doug Perrine/Innerspace Visions
73a: Tom McHugh/Photo Researchers
73b: Hults/Ricke
73c: Hults/Ricke
74–75: Kevin Schafer
76: E. R. Degginger/Color-Pic, Inc.
77a: E. R. Degginger/Color-Pic, Inc.
77b: David Liebman
77c: Karl H. Switak
78–79: R. D. Bartlett
79a (inset): James H. Robinson/Photo Researchers
79b: Tom Vezo/The Wildlife Collection
80: Karl H. Switak
81a: Robert W. Hansen
81b: Wiliam P. Leonard
82: E. R. Degginger/Color-Pic, Inc.
83a: R. D. Bartlett
83b: Brian Kenney
83c: Jeff Vanuga
84: E. R. Degginger/Color-Pic, Inc.
85a: Robert E. Barber
85b: David M. Dennis
86: M. P. L. Fogden/Bruce Coleman, Inc.
87a: Karl H. Switak
87b: Gerald & Buff Corsi/Focus on Nature, Inc.
87c: Karl H. Switak
88: Walt Anderson
89a: Gerald & Buff Corsi/Focus on Nature, Inc.
89b: David M. Dennis
89c: Karl H. Switak
90: Allen Blake Sheldon
91a: James H. Robinson
91b: David M. Dennis
91c (inset): Jack Dermid
91d: Allen Blake Sheldon
92: Wiliam P. Leonard
93a: Suzanne L. & Joseph T. Collins/CNAAR
93b: Robert W. Hansen
93c: James Simon/Photo Researchers
94: James H. Robinson
95a: R. W. Van Devender
95b: David M. Dennis
95c: David M. Dennis
96: E. R. Degginger/Color-Pic, Inc.
97a: Wiliam P. Leonard
97b: Karl H. Switak
98–99: Allen Blake Sheldon
99: Brian Kenney
100: Brian Kenney
101a: Allen Blake Sheldon
101b: William P. Leonard
101c: David M. Dennis

102–103: C. Allan Morgan
103: R. D. Bartlett
104–105: James H. Harding
105: E. R. Degginger/Color-Pic, Inc.
106: Allen Blake Sheldon
107a: David M. Dennis
107b: James H. Harding
107c: David M. Dennis
108: Allen Blake Sheldon
109a: Allen Blake Sheldon
109b: Suzanne L. Collins/CNAAR
109c: James H. Harding
110: Stephen G. Maka
111a: Brian Kenney
111b: Rob & Ann Simpson
111c: Allen Blake Sheldon
112: R. D. Bartlett
113a: Allen Blake Sheldon
113b: James Rowan
113c: R. W. Van Devender
114: Allen Blake Sheldon
115a: E. R. Degginger/Color-Pic, Inc.
115b: David M. Dennis
115c: Karl H. Switak
116: John Serrao
117a: David M. Dennis
117b: Suzanne L. & Joseph T. Collins/Photo Researchers
118–119: David M. Dennis
119: Suzanne L. Collins/CNAAR
120: Rob & Ann Simpson
121a: John M. Coffman
121b: Karl H. Switak
122: David M. Dennis
123a: R. W. Van Devender
123b: David M. Dennis
123c: Joseph T. Collins/Photo Researchers
124: Karl H. Switak
125a: Allen Blake Sheldon
125b: Suzanne L. Collins/CNAAR
126: Karl H. Switak
127a: Karl H. Switak
127b: Suzanne L. Collins/CNAAR
128: Karl H. Switak
129a: David M. Dennis
129b: R. W. Van Devender
130: Suzanne L. Collins/CNAAR
131a: Brian Kenney
131b: Karl H. Switak
131c: James H. Carmichael, Jr./Photo Researchers
132: Brian Kenney
133a: Karl H. Switak
133b: Allen Blake Sheldon
133c: Brian Kenney
134: Brian Kenney
135a: David M. Dennis
135b: Karl H. Switak
135c: R. D. Bartlett
136: Jack Dermid/Bruce Coleman, Inc.
137a: Brian Kenney

137b: Wiliam P. Leonard
137c: Karl H. Switak
138: David M. Dennis
139a: Brian Kenney
139b: Allen Blake Sheldon
139c: Allen Blake Sheldon
140: Allen Blake Sheldon
141a: Karl H. Switak
141b: Karl H. Switak
141c: Allen Blake Sheldon
142: David Liebman
143a: David M. Dennis
143b: E. R. Degginger/Color-Pic, Inc.
143c: Allen Blake Sheldon
144: E. R. Degginger/Color-Pic, Inc.
145a: David M. Dennis
145b: David M. Dennis
145c: Robert T. Zappalorti/Nature's Images
146: Kevin & Bethany Shank/Dogwood Ridge Photography
147a: Brian Kenney
147b: David M. Dennis
147c: Brian Kenney
148: R. D. Bartlett
149a: Allen Blake Sheldon
149b: E. R. Degginger/Color-Pic, Inc.
149c: Allen Blake Sheldon
150: Allen Blake Sheldon
150–151 (background): Michael H. Francis
152: Karl H. Switak
154: Dan Nedrelo
155: Charles W. Melton/The Wildlife Collection
157: James H. Robinson

*Photo Researchers, Inc.
60 East 56th Street
New York, NY 10022

Prepared and produced by
Chanticleer Press, Inc.

Publisher: Andrew Stewart
Founder: Paul Steiner

Chanticleer Staff:
Senior Editor-in-Chief: Amy K. Hughes
Senior Editor: Miriam Harris
Managing Editor: George Scott
Associate Editor: Michelle Bredeson
Editorial Interns: Abby Gordon, Morisa Kessler-Zacharias
Photo Director: Zan Carter
Photo Editor: Ruth Jeyaveeran
Associate Photo Editor: Jennifer McClanaghan
Rights and Permissions Manager: Alyssa Sachar
Photo Assistants: Leslie Fink, Sara Jones, Karin Murphy
Photo Intern: Marie Buendia
Art Director: Drew Stevens
Designer: Vincent Mejia
Assistant Designer: Anthony Liptak
Director of Production: Alicia Mills
Production Manager: Philip Pfeifer

Contributors:
Writer: John L. Behler
Consultant: James Harding
Photo Editor: Linda Patterson Eger, Artemis Picture Research Group, Inc.
Layout: Ann Bennett
Icons: Holly Kowitt

Scholastic Inc. Staff:
Editorial Director: Wendy Barish, Creative Director: David Saylor,
Managing Editor: Manuela Soares, Manufacturing Manager: Maria Aneiro

Original Series Design: Chic Simple Design